# The Curious History
## of *Bartholomew Fair*

# The Curious History
# of *Bartholomew Fair*

Frances Teague

*Lewisburg*
*Bucknell University Press*
*London and Toronto: Associated University Presses*

© 1985 by Associated University Presses, Inc.


Associated University Presses
440 Forsgate Drive
Cranbury, NJ 08512


Associated University Presses
25 Sicilian Avenue
London WC1A 2QH, England


Associated University Presses
2133 Royal Windsor Drive
Unit 1
Mississauga, Ontario
Canada L5J 1K5


**Library of Congress Cataloging in Publication Data**

Teague, Frances, 1949–
    The curious history of Bartholomew Fair.

    Bibliography: p.
    Includes index.
    1. Jonson, Ben, 1573?–1637.    Bartholomew Fair.
I. Title.
PR2606.T4   1985        822'.3        84-45006
ISBN 0-8387-5072-9


Printed in the United States of America

*This book is for my own Ben.*

# Contents

# Preface

THIS book extends and develops some of the ideas I had about *Bartholomew Fair* when I wrote my dissertation. That, however, was a straightforward analysis of staging, while this is a case study of a dramatic reputation's rise and fall and rise. In shifting the focus of my work, I received help from many generous people.

My first best thanks must go to John Velz who listened, corrected, and encouraged me throughout, and to Sarah Velz who worries with John. Chuck Lower's sensible advice is always worth hearing and I profited from his help and patience. Too many of my other colleagues offered information and advice for me to thank them individually. Though I do not list each one, I appreciate all.

William Park, George Walton Williams, Carol Carlisle, and Arthur Colby Sprague cheerfully shared their memories with me. Molly Sole of the Old Vic, Michael Bogdanov of the National Theatre, and the staffs at the Young Vic and the Bristol Old Vic all helped me track down information. I received special help and kindness from the staff at the Round House who made a stranger feel very welcome. George Parfitt and Peter Barnes had conversations with me that clarified my thinking about the play and about Jonson. Mary Free, William Blissett and Frank Warnke took time from hectic schedules to read and to advise.

Scholars are helpless without libraries. I was fortunate enough to work with some first-rate librarians here at the University of Georgia (especially the long-suffering Inter-Library Loan staff), at the Folger Shakespeare Library, at the British Museum, at the Nottingham Central Library, and at the Shakespeare Memorial Library in Stratford-upon-Avon. Scholarship also requires financial support. I am delighted to acknowledge the generosity of the American Council of Learned Societies, the University of Georgia Research Foundation, and the Department of English Research Fund, all of which provided grants so I could finish my research. I also thank the National Endowment for the Humanities for funding the Folger Institute on "Shakespeare in Performance," which brought me to the Folger at a crucial stage in footnote checking!

I also gratefully acknowledge permissions granted by the following publishers and organizations to reprint material: the Newcastle *Courier* for a theater review, the Old Vic Theatre for parts of the promptbook by George Devine, and the Round House in London for parts of the promptbook by Peter Barnes.

I always thank my own Ben. To him I owe the greatest debt of all.

Despite all the help I received, errors remain, and these I acknowledge mine. Like Jonson I must say:

> If in some things I dissent from others, whose *Wit, Industry, Diligence,* and *Iudgement* I looke up at, and admire: let me not therefore heare presently of Ingratitude, and Rashnesse. For I thanke those, that have taught me, and will ever: but yet dare not thinke the *scope* of their labour, and enquiry, was to envy their posterity, what they also could adde, and find out.
>
> If I erre, pardon me: *Nulla ars simul & inventa est, & absoluta.* I doe not desire to be equall to those that went before; but to have my reason examin'd with theirs, and so much faith to be given them, or me, as those shall evict. I am neither *Author,* or *Fautor* of any sect. I will have no man addict himself to mee; but if I have any thing right, defend it as Truth's, not mine (save as it conduceth to a common good.) It profits not me to have any man fence, or fight for me, to flourish, or take a side. Stand for *Truth,* and 'tis enough.

# The Curious History
## of *Bartholomew Fair*

# [ 1 ]

# Smithfield and Jonson

BEN Jonson is a writer of overshadowed greatness. E. B. Partridge has summed matters up succinctly:

> Could even Jonson have fashioned a more ironic fate than the one he found himself in—or, more precisely, the one we find him in? To write plays—when Shakespeare did? To write occasional poems for a circle that Donne moved in and wrote for? To be a critic—just after Sidney? To conceive of the heroic life—in the shadow of Spenser? To be concerned with the "advancement of Letters"—when there was a high government official who could write *The Advancement of Learning* and a *Novum Organum?*[1]

He achieved preeminence in one field—writing masques—but masques are a Renaissance art form about which most modern readers know little. And even here, Milton's *Comus* has diminished the praise that Jonson deserves. Despite his importance in English literature, Jonson remains underrated.

Even those critics who agree with T. S. Eliot that Jonson had "a large and unique view of life" fail to agree on what view of life Jonson had or what the scope of his plays might be.[2] Anyone who has worked with Jonson knows how widely critical reactions vary. To give just one example, several critics believe that Jonson's plays show his attitude toward religion. John S. Weld argues that Jonson's orthodox Christianity is central to *Volpone*, while Jackson Cope writes about the *un*orthodox use of blasphemy in *Bartholomew Fair*. Standing between these two views, Robert Knoll comments, "Jonson would seem to be the least pietistic of play-

13

wrights. He seems to have had a religious streak which he normally repressed."[3] This sort of critical unease recurs throughout commentaries on Jonson and his work.

If critics generally find Jonson and his plays difficult, it is no exaggeration to say that they find *Bartholomew Fair* impossible to agree on. In recent years its critical stock has risen, with some critics thinking it Jonson's greatest play. Their high opinion remains far from universal, however, and earlier critics, as a general rule, sneered at the play. Juxtaposing scraps of commentary about *Bartholomew Fair,* one finds the critics engaged in a game of vapors.

a. Compared with the moral issues in *Volpone* or *The Alchemist,* of course, those in *Bartholomew Fair* may appear slight—the mere follies of a fair instead of the absurd and terrible permutations of greed and lust.

b. *Bartholomew Fair* is undoubtedly Jonson's most ambitious attempt at a panoramic treatment of both the causes and effects of society's diseases, contamination, and impurity.

c. . . . it is, more emphatically than any other of Jonson's greater plays, of an age and not for all time.

d. . . . the culmination of the dramatist's comic art.

Cokes is a puzzle:

e. . . . we realize with a shock that Jonson is pronouncing a kind of blessing on the idiots of the world, on the gulls and naïfs, and their state of being perpetually deceived.

f. As the *reductio* of all the world's undirected, unexamined, unguarded silliness, this booby squire is ripe for the plucking, and he receives exactly what we might expect.

So is Ursula:

g. Ursula's being a woman and a personification of Smithfield assumes a meaning beyond the confines of one comedy.

h. The scene of the scalding allows us to identify [Ursula] the pig woman as *Ate, Discordia* herself.

i. Ursula . . . seems to be earth itself, the great Mother, Demeter, and Eve, a great goddess with all her shapes combined into one vast unshape—Ursa Major, the great bear which is also a wagon, appropriate enough to her function as a bawd.

j.    . . . an enormous exemplar of Eve, all fire and fat, a roaster of pigs. She is so hot that she sweats profusely, watering the ground in knots (like Falstaff's larding the earth). . . . She may even melt away into the first woman, a rib again, no doubt a pork rib.

k.    . . . there is . . . so much too much of everything that the whole thing becomes rather a wallow of which the Pig-woman and her pigs are all too truly symbol.

The play draws extreme reactions:

l.    . . . the hand-linked chain of the dance of life . . .

m.    . . . too accurate and too voluminous exposition of vulgar and vicious nature.

n.    . . . the tone of the play is notoriously genial.[4]

The views of its critics are notoriously scattered. They see the play as slight and panoramic, ephemeral and climactic. Cokes is a blessed naïf and a booby squire, while Ursula is . . . many things. If Ursula is a pantechnicon of literary symbols, the play itself is seen as a profound dance, a sermon against nature, and an exemplar of ge-niality.

Moreover, the criticism has curious gaps. Scholars rarely discuss Puritan reaction to the play after its revival in the Restoration. One can find excellent discussions of the play's importance in the Jon-son canon: some regard it as his greatest play, others as the begin-ning of his failure. But one finds little discussion or explanation of its theatrical success and even fewer attempts to set the play in a biographical context. Finally, critics rarely consider the relation of Jonson's play to the historical fair.

This study will attempt to fill in those gaps by telling the story of *Bartholomew Fair*. The context of the play, the milieu in which it was produced, and its adventures over three and a half centuries are of a piece with the play itself. If *Bartholomew Fair* is tasteless, vulgar, and uncontrolled, so are the things that have happened to it and around it. A record of the reactions to the play presents a picture of the playgoing public through several centuries (although at times this picture becomes a caricature). Such a history can also cast light on how and why Jonson's critical reputation has changed. Serious motives to the side, the story of *Bartholomew Fair* is worth telling simply because it is so lively.

In a sense, then, this study is the biography of a play. *David Copperfield* begins with a chapter simply titled, "I Am Born," but nowadays a proper biography begins with parents and family in order to look for clues to the hero's behavior in family patterns established long before his birth. But the parentage of *Bartholomew Fair* is difficult to establish. Although the play draws on a number of conventional situations—the disguised magistrate, the master thief, and the widow-hunters, for example—specific sources are hard to pinpoint. For instance, Jonson borrows from Juvenal's satires (as he had done in *Epicoene*) in Quarlous's attack on widows (1.3),[5] but the sentiments that Quarlous expresses come from Renaissance anti-feminist tracts as well as from classical Rome. Adam Overdo's disguise and investigation may refer to the actions of London's Lord Mayor, Sir Thomas Hayes, who roamed London in disguise to catch malefactors.[6] But Overdo's escapade may also come from the disguised Duke of Vienna in *Measure for Measure* or even from Haroun-Al-Rashid in *The Arabian Nights*. And tales about clever thieves abound through folklore.

Source hunting for this play has limited value. Even when a source is clearly identified, Jonson's reshaping tells one little about why the play elicits such varied reactions. For the purposes of a biographer, the sources are not the true progenitors. Instead one must turn to the Smithfield fair and to Ben Jonson's life.

Saint Bartholomew's Fair might be said to begin in the twelfth century with the founding of the Priory and Hospital of Saint Bartholomew. Like its literary descendant five centuries later, the fair has a history made lively by kings, clowns, and confidence men. While there is no evidence whatever to suggest that Jonson knew about the origins of the fair, an account of those origins shows some interesting coincidental features. The major ideas in *Bartholomew Fair* have historical counterparts in the history of the fair.

In 1133, Henry I granted his court jester, Rahere, a formal charter for an Augustinian priory honoring Saint Bartholomew, ten years after the priory had actually been founded.[7] Those ten years were busy ones for Rahere, for in them he turned a sickbed vision into concrete reality and won for his establishment popularity among Londoners. Rahere's accomplishment rested on his background as a jester; he knew how to wheedle and please before he found his religious vocation. While Jonson's play offers no court

jester for an audience's amusement, most of the fairground's inhabitants do make their living by amusing fairgoers and charming
them out of their money. Like the fairground vendors Lantern
Leatherhead and Joan Trash, Rahere made his living from the
public.

As a jester, Rahere had served Henry I well for many years,
entertaining the court with songs, jokes, and juggling—a skill at
which he was especially adept. He seems to have been an equally
skillful sycophant, for his earliest biographer, one of the priory's
monks, says Rahere got his start in life when "he began to haunt
the households of noblemen and the palaces of princes, where,
under every elbow of them, he spread their cushions with japes
and flatterings, delectably anointing their ears, by this manner to
draw to him their friendships."[8] In the 1120s, Rahere decided to go
on a pilgrimage to Rome to do penance for his sins, and while there
he contracted malarial fever and was expected to die.[9] Perhaps
Rahere flattered God and bargained with Him for recovery; perhaps the jester's conversion and repentance were sincere. In any
case, when Rahere regained his health, he had sworn that he would
return to London and establish a hospital for the poor.

This vow was strengthened by a vision of Saint Bartholomew
that Rahere said he had had. In this dream the Saint reminded
Rahere of his promise and told him precisely where to build a
priory and hospital; the area, which the Saint specified, was in
Smithfield. Once Rahere got back to London, he told his friends at
court of his vision. The Saint's selectivity created problems, for the
chosen piece of land was valuable and under the King's control.
The ground was contained within the King's Market, an official
marketplace which opened every Friday and which also served as
the site for an important annual cloth fair. Rahere could not simply
build his priory there; he had to receive the King's consent. But
Henry responded favorably to the jester's request, which was sup-
ported by Rahere's powerful friends, especially Richard de Bel-
meis. Thus Henry first granted Rahere the land and later gave him
an official charter; so from the outset Saint Bartholomew's has had
religious and economic significance, features which Jonson underlines in his play.

Of course, in Jonson's day the religious and economic stakes had
changed, just as the official religion had changed. Nonetheless, the
fair came under attack for its immorality, just as it had in Rahere's
day. Those who wished to close the fair for its profanity were
Puritans; opposed to them were the merchants at the Smithfield
fair, who wanted just as fervently to keep the fair open. The oppo-

sition between the Puritans' religious arguments and the merchants' economic arguments provides Jonson with a point of attack in his assault on Puritan hypocrisy. One of the arguments that the puppet Dionysius raises against the sectary, Rabbi Busy, is that Puritan tradesmen profited from the amusements that they claimed were sinful (5.5.73–83).[10] The conflict between religion and economics was perhaps inevitable given the successful nature of the fair, but Jonson's attack on Puritan hypocrisy, however well-grounded, ignores genuine moral problems.

The position of St. Bartholomew's, just outside London in an established market place, had always been convenient. It was in easy reach both of Londoners who came to the marketplace and of travellers who came to the cloth fair. Since the priory controlled the marketplace, it took part of the merchants' profits, as well as receiving any thank offerings from visitors. A certain notoriety proved profitable during the early years. The priory soon gained the reputation of being a place where miracles happened, and this fame improved its finances even more. There was a darker side to this reputation, for rumors also spread that Rahere arranged his own miracles; even members of Rahere's own household accused him of dishonesty.[11]

Henry Morley describes several such miracles in *A Memoir of Bartholomew Fair*.[12] In a typical example, a book once disappeared from the church. When Rahere heard the sad news, he remained calm and "took the harm with a soft heart patiently." The next morning he announced that he had had a dream which told him where the book was; he rode to the thief's house in the Jewish quarter of the city and found it straightaway. One can hardly help suspecting Rahere of hiding the book beforehand, but regardless of modern incredulity (and despite the carping of his own disbelieving monks), Rahere's fame as a miracle worker grew. In his day the public generally ignored disagreeable rumors in hope of receiving benefits for their offerings; in Jonson's day fairgoers ignored the fair's "enormities" and came to enjoy themselves. Certainly the ethics of the fairground characters had not improved. In the play Knockem and Whit cheerfully recruit prostitutes, Nightingale and Edgworth cut purses, while Trash and Leatherhead take Cokes's money without giving him the goods he pays for. Their actions are in the ethical tradition of Rahere's miracles: though Jonson's fair could promise no miracles, it did promise to satisfy fairgoers' desires.

In the Middle Ages, the public was especially generous to the priory during the annual three-day cloth fair—Bartholomew's Fair as they soon called it. During the fair, the usual trade was supplemented by cloth sellers from all over England who came to show their wares and sell to one another. In addition to the extra trade, booths opened which dispensed food and drink, while entertainers arrived to amuse the crowd. When England was Catholic, the priory was an active sponsor of the fair, and Rahere polished up his old juggling tricks to perform for the crowd and win alms for the priory. His successor, Thomas, also entertained the crowd; Thomas gained a reputation for reeling off extempore doggerel and occasionally delivered his sermons in verse.[13] In addition to such sanctioned participants at the medieval fair, whores, gamblers, and cutpurses made their appearance—by Jonson's day, the priory was gone, but the church and the less savoury characters remained.

Jonson's play depends on fairgoers who come to Bartholomew Fair in search of both sanctioned and illicit entertainment. By the fifth act all have left their pursuit of pigs or punks and been drawn in to watch the puppet show, an appropriate way to end a play about Bartholomew Fair. The Smithfield puppet plays probably began in the church, since European puppetry was first used to serve religion. (In fact, the word "marionette" means "little Mary," a reference to Christmas plays that first used puppets.)[14] The long tradition of English puppetry was acknowledged in 1573 by an order from the Lord Mayor of London that permitted Italian marionettes "to carry on their strange motions as in the past and from time immemorial."[15] One of the puppeteers' chief venues, from medieval days, was at Smithfield. Once again Jonson draws on a tradition of the fair.

He may also have drawn on his own experience, since Jonson possibly began his career by writing puppet plays. In *Satiromastix* (1601), Thomas Dekker attacked Jonson in the character of Horace; the play contains a number of personal comments about Jonson/Horace's appearance and experiences. At one point, Horace is called "the puppet-teacher" (4.3.174).[16] If Dekker meant to imply by this line that Jonson, like Lantern Leatherhead, had run puppet-shows, then another passage is immediately relevant to *Bartholomew Fair*'s puppets. In 1.2 Tucca says to Jonson/Horace:

Saist thou me so, olde Coale? come doo't then; yet tis no matter neither, Ile have thee in league first with these two rowly powlies: they shall be thy Damons and thou their Pithyasse; *Crispinus* shall giue thee

an olde cast Sattin suite, and *Demetrius* shall write thee a Scene or two,
in one of thy strong garlicke Comedies . . . (330–36)[17]

Old Cole, Damon and Pythias all appear in the fifth-act "strong
garlic" puppet play that ends *Bartholomew Fair.* Possibly Dekker
alludes in *Satiromastix* to an actual puppet play, which Jonson "the
puppet-teacher" had written in his earlier days, a puppet play
which he rewrote for *Bartholomew Fair.* This possibility is tantalizing; unfortunately, Dekker's allusion cannot be understood
with any certainty. We can, however, say that the puppets in
*Bartholomew Fair*'s fifth act serve religion, as the first Smithfield
puppets did, by attacking Busy who stands as a threat both to the
established religion and to the theater.

Puppets were not the only players in Smithfield. An illustration
in a priory manuscript shows a devil issuing from a hell's mouth to
cower at the Virgin's feet, a scene which suggests the priory offered miracle plays.[18] Records survive to show that mystery plays
were performed. In 1390 or 1391 the guild of St. Nicholas (parish
clerks) put on a play for Richard II at Skinner's Well (near
Smithfield); in 1409 Richard's deposer, Henry IV, watched the
clerks perform "Matter from the World's Creation."[19]

These first command performances for royalty raise two points:
the fair's importance and its curious legal position. First of all, the
kings' presence marks the importance that the early fair had so-
cially as well as economically. In the Middle Ages, the appeal of the
fair was not limited to the lower and middle classes; fairgoers came
from all ranks of society and might be said to provide a microcosm
of that society. This feature of the fair had changed by 1614, since
James I's dislike of crowds was enough to keep him away from
Smithfield. Grace reflects this change in fashion when she remarks,

Truly, I have no such fancy to the Fair, nor ambition to see it; there's
none goes thither of any quality or fashion. (1.5.121–22)

Though the king did not attend the fair, the Lord Mayor, sheriffs,
and aldermen of London put in a ceremonial appearance, opening
the fair and warning its participants to obey the law. (Jonson's
character, Puppy, has come to the fair to wrestle before the Lord
Mayor; 4.3.105–6.)[20]

This opening-day proclamation raises a second point: the curious legal position of the fair. In a way, the fair, which cut across
society, was beyond the normal rules of that society. The kings

were there as spectators rather than figures of authority. If a king had granted the franchise of a fair, he could not take it back; like a commonly used road on private property, the public gained some rights in it and it could not be closed by fiat.[21] Moreover the fairs had their own courts to try merchants accused of cheating customers and thieves who stole from merchants. These courts were called *Pieds Poudres* or Courts of the Dusty Feet, a reference to the road conditions travellers met on their way to the fair.[22] This name was soon Anglicized to Pie Powders Court, the name Jonson uses in his play. Pie Powders tried all cases that involved the commerce of the fair, and it tried such cases before a jury of traders from the fair. Since the court only operated during the annual fair, a case could be held over to the next year, but it could not be turned over to another court for trial. (In Jonson's *Bartholomew Fair*, when Adam Overdo decides to spend a day in disguise at the fair, leaving his court to fend for itself, his action means that, for one day of the fair, not even this peculiar court was in session.)

E. B. Partridge has remarked that ". . . the Fair gradually became a peculiar nexus of religion, trade, and pleasure."[23] But the connections among the church, the traders, and the entertainers did not come into being gradually; they were there all along. Rahere, with his juggling and his eye to the main chance, embodied them. The connections had intensified by Jonson's day and, not surprisingly, he uses this nexus to unify his play.

The religious controversy began with Rahere and his dubious miracles, but it continued throughout the fair's history. After Rahere established his priory, it continued until Henry VIII broke with the Roman Catholic Church. Although Saint Bartholomew's Hospital survived into the new dispensation (and, of course, still survives today), the priory and the rights it had over the fair were turned over to secular authority.[24] When Jonson wrote, he was simply making use of the most recent contretemps: first, the St. Bartholomew's Day Massacre and second, the Puritan attacks.

Under the Church of England, St. Bartholomew's Day remained important.[25] On August 24, 1572, in France, the long simmering hostility against the Huguenots boiled over into violence. Catholic soldiers, aided by the citizens of Paris, killed every Huguenot who could be found. Men, women, and children were slaughtered. Dreadful as this massacre was, worse came the following day and it grew out of an accident of nature. On the morning of August 25, a hawthorn tree blossomed in a churchyard, months out of season. The tree's blooms were a miracle, thought the clerics, a sign from God sanctioning the slaughter. They ordered the church bells rung to mark the occasion, but when the ringing began, the Catholic populace interpreted the sounds as a sign that they should recommence killing Huguenots. From Paris the killing spread. While the final total of deaths cannot be given accurately, a conservative estimate is that 2,000 Protestants were killed in Paris and 5,000 in other parts of France.

The impact that the massacre of Saint Bartholomew's Day had on the rest of Europe was enormous. Catholics rejoiced. The devout Catholic, Philip II of Spain, is supposed to have smiled in public only once—when he heard of the Massacre. Pope Gregory XIII held a thanksgiving mass. In Protestant countries such as England, however, the public mourned the dead Huguenots and regarded their murders with horror. The Scots called for an equally horrendous slaughter of Catholics—a massacre that was, fortunately, stopped by the government. In 1587, fifteen years later, when Mary Queen of Scots was sentenced to death by the English, the French government sent Elizabeth a letter interceding for Mary. Elizabeth answered scornfully that such a plea came poorly from a people who had committed the Massacre of Saint Bartholomew's Day. In commemoration of the event, many London booksellers displayed only Bibles in their windows on August 24 in following years.[26] August 24 was the day of the fair, but for the English it also epitomized the conflict between Catholics and Protestants.

Yet Jonson mentioned the massacre only once in his play. Overdo begs Wasp to stop beating him:

Hold thy hand, child of wrath and heir of anger. Make it not Childermass day in thy fury, or the feast of the French Barthol'mew, parent of the massacre. (2.6.133ff.)

This absence of allusions at first seems odd, especially when one considers Rabbi Busy's outbursts of fervor. Even Latin tags set Busy off against Papists (4.6.93), but the massacre goes unmentioned. This omission probably stems from the fact that Jonson's play is not concerned with the conflict of Catholic against Protestant but with a new conflict, Puritan against the rest of English society, though the omission may also reflect Jonson's personal religious convictions.

By 1614, the fashion in religious controversy had changed. The stage-keeper might long for "a well-educated ape to come over the chain for the King of England and back again for the Prince, and sit still on his arse for the Pope and the King of Spain" (Induction, 15–17), but the stagekeeper's taste is hopelessly old-fashioned. Jonson is more interested in the Puritans who would shut down the theaters. He had attacked them in *The Alchemist* and returned to the attack in *Bartholomew Fair.* Jonson's position is clear: he refuses to acknowledge that Puritanism has any religious validity.[27] In *Bartholomew Fair,* the word "Puritan" is just another name for "hypocrite."

Jonson may have omitted references to the massacre for more personal reasons as well. Although he was hostile to Puritanism, he might have been ambivalent about the conflict between Anglicans and Catholics. Jonson was raised in an Anglican household (his dead father was a clergyman who had been persecuted by Mary Tudor), but he came to reject the Church of England.[28] In 1598 Jonson converted to Catholicism while in prison. He returned to the Anglican Church in 1610, but his experience must have tempered his response to the horror stories of the Bartholomew's Day Massacre. Another experience suggests that he had the reputation of being a fair-minded observer of religious controversy. In 1612 Jonson travelled to France as a tutor to Sir Walter Raleigh's son. During this trip he was invited to serve as an official witness at a formal debate in which a Catholic, M. D. Smith, and a Protestant, Daniel Featley, argued for the relative merits of their beliefs.[29] (Jonson's *Conversations with Drummond* suggests that most of this trip abroad was less sedate. Possibly the relationship between Wasp and Cokes reflects his experience with ebullient Wat Raleigh.)[30] Although events in Jonson's life show his involvement with religion—especially his deep concern with the relative merits of Anglican and Catholic belief—such issues rarely come up in his plays. When it came to religion, Jonson was no rabble-rouser.

However, religious controversy runs throughout the history of the Smithfield fair and Jonson includes religious questions in his attack on Busy. He includes trade and pleasure as well; again, he treats these topics in a way congruous with the traditions of Bartholomew Fair. To begin with, the distinction between trade and pleasure is a misleading one with regard to Smithfield. From the earliest days, the fairgrounds offered food and entertainment for the cloth-traders' pleasure. As the fair went on, the entertainment assumed even greater importance and became a significant economic element, earning a niche in the fair's hierarchy.

At the top of this hierarchy one would place the Pie Powders court which provided the fair's chief authority. Next came the major merchants who bought and sold, the cloth traders. The smaller businesses, which served the traders by amusing and feeding them, made up the third level; they drew in other customers from the city who came to see the sights and eat the famous Bartholomew pigs. The final level of "traders" consisted of those who sought their profits from crime—prostitutes and thieves.

Each level of the trade-pleasure hierarchy is included in Jonson's play. Most of the characters fit the third and fourth levels, of course, and the overlap between these two levels can be seen in Ursula or Knock'em. Trouble-all and the three watchmen join with Justice Adam Overdo to represent authority within the fair; Overdo's abandonment of authority, Trouble-all's madness, and the watchmen's incompetence provide an index to the worth of that authority. The second level of the hierarchy has only one character in *Bartholomew Fair*—Nordern the Clothier.

The scanting of the second level seems odd. Just as Jonson generally ignores the Bartholomew Day Massacre, he seems to overlook the cloth market which occasions the rest of the fair. Once again, the explanation for the omission may lie in Jonson's background.

There are two ways that Jonson might have known the fair. Obviously he had gone to see the sights. As a boy Jonson lived only a mile or so from Smithfield, in easy walking distance;[31] most of his life he would have been able to attend the fair. Though Jonson had been a fairgoer, he may have been a puppeteer as well. (Certainly if he were not a puppeteer, the allusions to puppetry in Dekker's *Satiromastrix* make little sense.) As a puppeteer Jonson would have seen a different side of the fair. His play suggests that those participants at the third level were not above dishonesty when it suited their purposes and they they were very conscious of Pie Powders Court. They would not, however, care much about the cloth fair except insofar as it sent them customers. In this case, *Bartholomew Fair* may reflect Jonson's own experience with the fair and his own taste in amusements.

While Jonson must have enjoyed himself at the fair, the more outrageous exhibits and behavior disgusted him. He might laugh at the puppet shows, even remember past experiences working with puppets, but he was angry and complained when "The Puppets [were] seene . . . in despight of the Players."[32] One cannot deny his affection for the fair; it comes through clearly in his play. Jonson never overrated it and he felt contempt for those who did, yet he knew that he himself overrated some things which were finally of

little more importance than a summer's fair. Wry self-amusement
mixes with contempt in this statement from *Discoveries:*

> *What* petty things they are, wee wonder at? like children, that esteeme
> every trifle, and preferre a *Fairing* before their Fathers: what difference
> is betweene us, and them? but that we are dearer Fooles, Cocks-
> combes, at a higher rate? They are pleas'd with Cockleshels, Whistles,
> Hobby-horses, and such like: wee with Statues, marble Pillars, Pic-
> tures, guilded Roofes, where under-neath is Lath, and Lyme; perhaps
> Lome. Yet, wee take pleasure in the lye, and are glad, we can cousen
> our selves.[33]

This attitude toward the fair is a complex one, raising aesthetic and
ethical questions.

The attitude he expresses towards fairs, and more pretentious
spectacles as well, at first seems extreme. Modern readers may be
taken aback when Jonson bluntly dismisses elaborate scenery as a
lie and says that anyone enjoying it cozens himself. But this evaluation is qualified by his unstated belief in the central Horatian
principle: all his life Jonson maintained that the artist (of the fairground, the theater, the court) ought to provide the spectator with
pleasure *and profit.* Discussing the relationship between poetry and
picture, Jonson writes, "*Poetry* and *Picture* are Arts of a like nature; and both are busie about imitation. . . . They both behold
pleasure, and profit, as their common Object; but should abstaine
from all base pleasures, lest they should erre from their end; and
while they seeke to better mens minds, destroy their manners."[34]
This conviction, that any form of art must simultaneously enter-
tain and teach, leads Jonson to his dissatisfaction with "Lath . . .
Lyme . . . Lome." The external appearance of these, like the external appearance of the fair, is misleading, yet one takes pleasure in
it. But this is only half of what is needed.

The pleasure must come not only from viewing rich things (marble statues, pillars, etc.) but also from discerning their essentially
false nature. If a spectator takes pleasure in the lie, yet also *in-
creases* his discernment—his ability to distinguish—all is well.
However, feeling pleasure at misleading appearance becomes foolish when the spectator's discernment is weak and inadequate.
What Jonson questions in this passage on a fair is whether one can
"profit" from mistaking falsehood for reality, whether one can
receive instruction as well as "take pleasure in the lye." This question recurs throughout his work: sometimes his characters cozen

each other, and sometimes, as in *Epicoene,* he works through his characters to cozen the audience. But in these cases he is eager to show the drawbacks of confusing marble with lath and lime; profit comes in learning to distinguish.

The most forceful part of this passage is not Jonson's observation that appearance can be misleading. More important is Jonson's recognition that foolishness is universal. *Everyone* is a "petty thing"; *all* are "like children." Those who set too high a value on fine settings are like those who overrate fairground stalls; the only difference is that the former are "dearer Fooles, Cockscombes, at a higher rate." Jonson is not only acknowledging human fallibility; he does something more difficult by including himself in his own strictures.

Jonson's use of "we" is not simply a rhetorical device. He is, explicitly, including himself in his list of fools. Moreover, he may be referring to a personal concern. When he speaks of "Statues, marble Pillars, Pictures, guilded Roofes, where underneath is Lath and Lyme; perhaps Lome," he is describing the sort of scenery Inigo Jones would prepare for one of their elaborate court masques. Jones seems to have thought his share of this work was at least as important as Jonson's, if not of paramount importance.[35] But Jonson's commitment was always to poetry (the pen) rather than picture (the pencil); he says, ". . . of the two, the Pen is more noble, than the Pencill. For that [i.e. the Pen] can speake to the Understanding; the other, but to the Sense."[36] Inevitably the two men argued.

Although Jonson feuded with Jones over the elaborate scenery and effects, he was nonetheless concerned about the appearance of his masques (and presumably his plays). He published his notes on the appearance of the characters in several masques and had read widely in emblematic literature.[37] In *Discoveries,* he voiced his concern about appearance: "*Whosoever* loves not *Picture* is injurious to Truth: and all the wisdome of *Poetry.*"[38] The external appearance must lead to truth and wisdom; the words of the poet guide the understanding in this process. Anyone who forgets this process, even Jonson, is a "Foole, Cockscombe."

Jonson's play about the fair is less elaborate scenically than any of his masques. Nonetheless it is a play about misleading appearance and its characters do mistake the value of the fair. Moreover, as a comedy, *Bartholomew Fair* has special responsibilities. Comedy, Jonson felt, is the form of poesy closest to oratory and rhetoric; comic excellence lies in "moving the minds of men, and

stirring of affections."[39] In this passage of *Discoveries* Jonson returns to the relationship between picture and poetry:

> What figure of a Body was *Lysippus* ever able to forme with his Graver,
> or *Apelles* to paint with his Pencill, as the Comedy to life expresseth so
> many and various affections of the minde? There shall the Spectator see
> some, insulting with Joy; others, fretting with Melancholy; raging with
> Anger; mad with Love; boiling with Avarice; undone with Riot; tor-
> tur'd with expectation; consum'd with feare: no perturbation in com-
> mon life, but the Orator findes an example of it in the Scene.[40]

Jonson's description of what a spectator at a comedy might see
would do very well for a description of *Bartholomew Fair.*
   It is, then, a play which draws upon Jonson's personal values as
well as his personal life. Ben Jonson grew up with Bartholomew
Fair; as a mature artist, he struggled with an aesthetic and ethical
problem which the fair epitomized.
   But the play was a personal matter in other ways as well. Jonson
wrote his play as a friend and he wrote for friends. Nathan Field,
who played in *Bartholomew Fair,* was one of Jonson's closest
friends. Jonson told William Drummond that "Nid field was his
Schollar & he had read to him the Satyres of Horace & Some
Epigrames of Martiall";[41] since Field began acting when he was
only thirteen, Jonson may well have tried to introduce the young
actor to classical authors. Jonson's servant and secretary, Richard
Brome, was also a friend and protégé; he seems to have worked
with Jonson, helping to produce the play.[42] Brome later left Jonson's service, but never his patronage; he had a successful career as
a playwright himself. John Aubrey is not a reliable source, but his
remark that "Ben Jonson was never a good actor, but an excellent
instructor" has the ring of truth.[43] Both Field and Brome learned
from Jonson and benefited from his teaching. When the three men
worked together on *Bartholomew Fair,* they, at least, must have
received pleasure and profit from this collaboration.
   Jonson's relations with the rest of the company of Lady
Elizabeth's Men were also good. The company's personnel included most of the members of the Children of the Queen's Revels, which had successfully produced *Epicoene* a few years before.[44] (Philip Henslowe, who had given Jonson his first work as a
playwright, had merged the two companies in 1613.)[45] As a result,
Jonson knew many of the actors personally and presumably approved of their work. The production was a crucial one for the

Lady Elizabeth's Men. Thanks to Henslowe's merger, the company was relatively new and was putting on Jonson's play in their new theater, the Hope. The theater needed a paying audience, the company needed a public, and *Bartholomew Fair* could provide both. Although the play and the theater were successful, the company was not. In the next two years the Lady Elizabeth's Men lost eight of their actors: Field, Joseph Taylor, Robert Benfield, Robert Hamlen, William Barksted, Robert Pallant, Emanuel Reade, and Thomas Basse. The Lady Elizabeth's Men soon became a provincial company only, touring the countryside until 1622 when they returned to the London theaters.

In the autumn of 1614, however, the company's prospects were auspicious. Jonson was a popular playwright, Field a popular actor. Perhaps word had reached the court that Jonson, a favorite of King James, had included an attack on the troublesome Puritans in his new play, an attack even stronger than the one in *The Alchemist*. In any case, an invitation went out to the Lady Elizabeth's Men: on November 1, the night after the play opened at the Hope, they were to perform before the king.

This invitation meant extra work in preparing the play. Jonson probably scrutinized his play a bit more closely for lines that might offend the King. After Jonson finished going over his play, he wrote a prologue and an epilogue complimenting the King appropriately. Meanwhile the company's stage manager had to arrange for funds from the court to pay the added costs of a second performance; next he had to arrange a second stage set for the performance before the King. A record of this financial arrangement remains in an account book authorizing payment for "Canvas for the Boothes and other necessaries for a play called Bartholomewe Faire."[46]

But finally the work of preparation ended. "A play called Bartholomewe Faire" was ready for the public.

## [ 2 ]

# The Effect of *Bartholemew Fair*

THE history of the Smithfield fair and Jonson's own connections with the fair certainly bring one closer to an understanding of *Bartholomew Fair.* But understanding the original circumstances of the production is important as well. In fact, one might guess how important this question is from the fact that three scholars—William Armstrong, Brian Parker, and Eugene Waith—have suggested reconstructions of the staging.[1] (I find Waith's the most convincing of these three, and that is the one I will refer to in my discussion. I should add, however, that the points I make are congruous with the other stagings.) One may find that in the process of reconstructing the staging—whether at the Hope, where the play opened, or at court, where it was performed the next night—a more important question is overlooked, one that lies at the heart of much of the controversy about *Bartholomew Fair.* What was the *effect* of the staging?

If we could, in some way, know how the audiences at the Hope and at court understood the play, the effect it had on them, we would know much more about how Jonson intended to work on a stage. This is not to say that all theatrical effects are intentional ones, but certainly some are. Jonson was not a haphazard craftsman, but rather one who carefully planned his drama and who had clear expectations about what his plays ought to do to an audience. Several problems of effect deserve especially close study. The first of these is the troubling Induction and the intended effect that its theatrical rhetoric had on its initial audiences at the Hope and at court. A second problem is the play's curious structure, with its lack of a central character around whom the plot can coalesce; how did Jonson expect his audience to understand this structure? Finally, of course, one must decide what to make of Jonson's ambiguous ending: is it supposed to be cynical or genial? slight or profound?

In *Bartholomew Fair* Jonson seems highly conscious of the different audiences present on the first afternoon and second night. The complimentary prologue is appropriate to the court audience, but it has no point for the Hope's audience. Sections of his Induction are clearly aimed at the public spectators, rather than royal taste. For example, comments on the theater's filthy condition or the admission price are intended only for the Hope audience, since the court audience would find such comments obscure, even rude. Probably the court production omitted these lines, as the Hope production omitted the prologue.

William Blissett has even suggested that Jonson left the entire Induction out of the court production.[2] The Book-holder introduces Jonson's contract with the spectators by the line, "Gentlemen, not for want of a prologue, but by way of a new one, I am sent out to you here with a scrivener and certain articles drawn out in haste between our author and you . . ." (Induction, 51–54). The phrase "not for want of a prologue" is ambiguous: does the Book-holder mean that the contract will *substitute* for a prologue or that the contract is offered *in addition* to a prologue? Since the court performance had a prologue and the Hope performance evidently did not (none survives), this line may be deliberately ambiguous and intended for both performances. (Jonson's use of prologue and an Induction seems pointlessly redundant, yet he had used both devices in *Cynthia's Revels* and *The Poetaster.*) One indication that Jonson intended at least part of the Induction for a court performance is that it includes jokes and exposition more suitable for a court audience than a public one.

Jonson directs the joke about those who "will swear *Jeronimo* and *Andronicus* are the best plays yet" against the public audience's old-fashioned taste, and the court audience might well laugh at such unsophisticated attitudes. His warnings about the "state-decipherer, or politic picklock" also seem intended for the court audiences, since Jonson's reputation for controversy is the heart of the joke, a reputation that James and his court were far more likely to care—and worry—about than the public audience was. Those spectators at the Hope could understand it, of course, if they recalled that Jonson went to prison for both *The Isle of Dogs* (1597) and *Eastward Ho!* (1605) and was investigated for *Epicoene*

(1609).³ Some of Jonson's jokes do not exclude either audience; instead they are double-edged, carrying definite and different meanings to each group.

Within the play, the satire on the Puritans is one such double-edged joke. Both the audiences disliked the Puritans: those at the Hope would recognize Rabbi Busy as one of a group which was trying to shut down the theaters, and those at court would see him as one of the religious dissidents who attacked the royal powers. In either case, Busy threatens both of the worlds outside the play, though those worlds differ widely. Again, jokes about the yearning for roast pig, the foolish magistrate, and tobacco work for both worlds. The public audience knew these things at first hand. They had eaten roast pig, suffered from foolish magistrates, put up with (or enjoyed) clouds of tobacco smoke. Each item was part of their daily life. At court, where James determined conduct and taste, the audience also recognized these three topics. James disliked pork, scolded foolish magistrates, and had published *A Counterblaste to Tobacco* (1604).⁴ In both cases, the jokes refer to everyday life, whether in the streets of London or the halls of Westminster.

The Stagekeeper's animadversions on Jonson's account of Smithfield work differently. Most of the audience at the Hope had gone to the fair. What the Stagekeeper says amuses them because they can compare it to their personal experiences. However, the most important member of the court audience had *not* been to Smithfield; that audience surely held others besides James who knew the fair only by hearsay. Nonetheless, they would not find the Stagekeeper's remarks pointless or puzzling. For this segment of the court audience, the Stagekeeper's comments become necessary exposition, giving them the background they will need to understand the play. Moreover, anyone who thinks that what Jonson does is vulgar or tasteless need only listen to the Stagekeeper to learn that Jonson has provided a cleaned-up version of Bartholomew Fair. He has left out most of the bullies, thieves, and whores in his version. The Stagekeeper asks:

> Would not a fine pump upon the stage ha' done well for a property now? And a punk set under upon her head, with her stern upward, and ha' been soused by my witty young masters a' the Inns o' Court? What think you o' this for a show now? (Induction, 28–32)

His questions suggest that the audience should consider Jonson's fair as subdued, even decorous, by comparison to the real fair.

Jonson tries to control audience response to his play—always a tricky business—by the way he uses the Stagekeeper. Both the royal prologue and the Induction suggest that Jonson feared two charges. First of all, his audience might find *Bartholomew Fair* vulgar or indecorous. In the prologue when Jonson tells the king to expect "such place, such men, such language and such ware" as are suited to Smithfield, he tries to forestall complaints about the tone of his play. Similarly, the Induction warns against any "such as shall so desperately or ambitiously play the fool by his place aforesaid, to challenge the author of scurrility because the language somewhere savors of Smithfield, the booth, and the pig-broth; or of profaneness because a madman cries, 'God quit you,' or 'bless you'" (131–35).

A second possible charge is that *Bartholomew Fair* is too topical. Both the prologue and the Induction mock those who take Jonson's satire too personally and see themselves as his target. In the prologue Jonson maintains that his play is "without particular wrong, / Or just complaint of any private man / Who of himself or shall think well or can. . . ," while his Induction warns against "any state-decipherer, or politic picklock of the scene, so solemnly ridiculous as to search out who was meant by the gingerbread-woman, who by the hobbyhorse-man, who by the costermonger, nay, who by their wares" (122–25). The fact that Jonson repeats his warnings in the prologue and Induction indicates his concern with the oversolemn, oversensitive members of both audiences; but his chief tool for manipulating response is the Stagekeeper, who appears only in the Induction. His speech begins the release of tension into laughter when the audience recognizes him as an actor speaking Jonson's lines; the release continues with the contract. Furthermore, his warning that the spectators will not care for the play establishes him as a clod. When the audience laughs at him, they repudiate him; conversely, by laughing at the mock contract, they sanction it. Finally, those who find that the play lacks decorum and those who find its satire too pointed are caught in a double bind by the Stagekeeper's complaints. If they disagree with him, they accept Jonson's play. But if they agree, they align themselves with his argument that Jonson has cleaned up the fair too thoroughly and that his play has moved too far from a naturalistic presentation. The Stagekeeper's position is irreconcilable with objections about "scurrility" and "politic picklocks."

A shift in emphasis occurs from the earlier plays, which viewed man as actor, to *Bartholomew Fair*, which views man as spectator. Jonson shows this concern with the spectator when he asks the audience to agree to a contract, thus forcing the relationship between actors and audience, which usually remains tacit, into explicitness. The Lady Elizabeth's Men will try to provide entertainment, and possibly enlightenment, while the audience will not make a negative judgment on the play either before they see it or without good reason. Yet this agreement is not so open as it seems: Jonson keeps careful control over it. The spectators may ally themselves either with the ignorant Stagekeeper who makes ridiculous arguments against the company or else with the witty playwright who pays them the compliment of gracefully seeking their favor.

The audience is prevented from making a negative prejudgment because they agree to the contract *and* because Jonson has carefully forestalled their objections to his play. Every complaint the Stagekeeper makes is effectively undercut. The Induction starts with the Stagekeeper saying that Jonson is ignorant about the theater and complaining, "He has not hit the humors, he does not know 'em" (10–11). But it was Jonson who had given theater the comedy of humors; of course he would "know 'em," and know them better than any other playwright. The Stagekeeper then begins his catalogue of all the things the play should have, but lacks. Each of his charges is later countered by the contract, which explains Jonson's substitutions:

> Instead of a little Davy to take toll o' the bawds, the author doth promise a strutting horse-courser with a leer drunkard, two or three to attend him in as good equipage as you would wish. And then for Kindheart, the tooth-drawer, a fine oily pig-woman with her tapster to bid you welcome, and a consort of roarers for music. A wise justice of peace *meditant,* instead of a juggler with an ape. A civil cutpurse *searchant.* A sweet singer of ballads *allurant:* and as fresh an hypocrite as ever was broached *rampant.* (Induction, 105–13)

The list of more wholesome substitutions answers all of the Stagekeeper's claims of deficiency and whets the audience's appetite for the play that will follow.

However, the Stagekeeper does name one thing which the contract cannot counter when he complains that the company has no one so good as the great clown, Richard Tarleton. The company was a comparatively new one; the leading actor, Nathan Field, had joined the company that year and, although he was well-known, he was no Burbage—or Tarleton. The Stagekeeper says:

> Ho! an' that man Tarleton had lived to have played in *Barthol'mew Fair,* you should ha' seen him ha' come in, and ha' been cozened i' the cloth-quarter, so finely! And Adams the rogue, ha' leaped and capered

upon him, and ha' dealt his vermin about as though they cost him nothing. And then a substantial watch to ha' stol'n in upon 'em, and taken 'em away with mistaking words, as the fashion is in the stage-practice. (Induction, 33–39)

To some extent, this speech is a gibe at unsophisticated taste which prefers slapstick to Jonsonian wit; nonetheless, Jonson seems to acknowledge some force to these complaints since he offers in his play each piece of stage business that the Stagekeeper outlines. Coke loses his clothes in 4.2, much as Tarleton claimed to have lost his at the cloth fair. Although Adams cannot beat Tarleton, Jonson does give marginal stage directions for his characters to fight six times in the play.[5] And as in the Stagekeeper's description, the three watchmen engage in Dogberry-like dialogue with Trouble-all as they lock Justice Overdo in the stocks.

*Bartholomew Fair* is a consciously theatrical play in many ways, and that conscious theatricality may well be Jonson's way of bridging the gap between his two audiences. Rather than aiming the play at a particular audience, or setting his play in the world of the Hope or the court, he presents the fairground world, the world of the professional entertainer. Jonson's grumpy complaint in *Discoveries* that "the Puppets are seene now in despight of the Players"[6] suggests that he thought the spectrum of popular entertainment extended from the fairground to the playhouse, although the performances at the playhouse were higher in quality and deserved a bigger audience. In his play, with both puppets and actors performing, he presents this third world, the world as theater, to his audiences.

The force of the Induction's theatrical rhetoric comes from Jonson's concern with his spectators and his understanding of their relationship to the actors they watch. Yet Jonson's concern with man as spectator has another dimension in *Bartholomew Fair*. In his earlier plays he had concentrated on man as actor; his actors played actors in plays within plays. In *Bartholomew Fair*, half the characters have come to the fair as spectators, to see the fun. Yet the fairground characters also act as spectators, for they want to make money unobtrusively; publicity would destroy them, so they watch their customers more closely than they themselves are watched. A prime example is the pocket-picking scene. In 3.5, Cokes watches Nightingale's performance and Nightingale keeps a lookout for Edgworth. Cokes performs also, showing off his purse for the benefit of Edgworth, who finally steals it. Edgworth's performance as cutpurse is watched by another audience, Quarlous and Winwife, and they in turn are watched by the playhouse spectators. The characters spend their time either gawking, like Cokes, or trying to avoid the attention of others, like Lantern Leatherhead in 5.3. A protagonist who watches others or seeks a passive role is inherently undramatic. Jonson works around this difficulty through the play's structure.

Instead of a unified structure of the sort found in *Volpone*, Jonson has carried the episodic structure of *The Alchemist* one step further. In *Volpone*, the main plot and the subplot run parallel to each other, but they rarely overlap. In each line of action, one event causes another; the plots are orderly. However, in *The Alchemist*, one line of action is tangled with another until the grand sorting-out at the end of the play. The three cheats must struggle to keep each transaction separate if they are to survive, but the force of circumstances works to combine the events of one episode with those of another. Similarly, in *Bartholomew Fair* all of the characters come to the fair for different reasons, and their encounters with each other and the fairground characters create the increasingly complex plot. In *The Alchemist* the three rogues are performers and protagonists who are set against the credulous world; in *Bartholomew Fair* only the wooden puppets refuse the role of spectator and are willing to stand up before the world.

*Bartholomew Fair* has no character to serve as a protagonist. Insofar as the play has any central figure around whom events coalesce, it is the fair itself. For it is the fair which remains before the audience's eyes in the last four acts, the fair which draws together characters as diverse as Punk Alice and Mistress Overdo, the fair which rules every man's actions. Ultimately one's understanding of the play depends on one's understanding of the fair. But this fact creates a critical problem. In a play which has a human protagonist, one may study his character by analyzing the things he says or does and what others say about or to him. One can only study the fair through its appearance on stage and what the other characters tell us about it. An understanding of the fair depends on its theatrical physiognomy.

The first act of *Bartholomew Fair* is set on a bare stage. No stage furniture is mentioned, and the action probably takes place in the street before Littlewit's house (the locale is left ambiguous). In this act Jonson concentrates on people and provides the audience with the exposition necessary for the rest of the play; the act establishes who the characters are (an important preliminary in a play as complex as *Bartholomew Fair*) and what each of them hopes to find at the fair. The characters themselves provide a kind of setting, for everyone in the first act wants something he does not have. John and Win Littlewit want to see John's puppet play and to escape Puritan restraints in having a good time; Dame Purecraft, Winwife, and Grace all want to get married; Quarlous wants sport; Wasp wants to quarrel; Busy wants to eat and prophesy; and Dame Overdo simply wants to have a serene existence in which everyone agrees. Cokes shares his name, Bartholomew, with the fair, and he wants "his" fair.

The bare stage of act 1 is appropriate, then, for the action makes clear that the ordinary world is a deprived world, empty of the things which will satisfy a character's wishes. In contrast, the fair itself, with its jumble of things, is a magic place, a place where wishes can, and do, come true. The stage is filled with the world in miniature in acts 2 through 4, and anything one wants can be found there.

At the beginning of act 2, the stage is still empty when Adam Overdo appears to give his speech about the fair's "yearly enormities" and to make his wish—that he will learn the truth about the fair. As he speaks, the stage fills up. Ursula and Mooncalf place the largest booth upstage center at the same time as Lantern Leatherhead sets up his smaller hobbyhorse booth at stage left. Between the two booths Joan Trash puts her stool and gingerbread stand, probably a small table. At stage left, the stocks are placed, either by supernumeraries or by the watchmen, Haggis, Bristle, and Poacher. When Overdo ends his soliloquy, Joan Trash and Lantern Leatherhead begin quarrelling over their space, only to break off as the fairgoers arrive. Leatherhead cries to them, "What do you lack?" a cry that echoes through the rest of the play, while Joan Trash and the Costermonger appeal to their appetites with gingerbread and pears. Behind the action, Nightingale hawks his ballads and sings:

> Hey, now the Fair's a filling!
> O, for a tune to startle
> The birds o' the booths here billing
> Yearly with old Saint Bartle!
>
> (2.2.32–35)

The scene looks like John Newberry's *Cries of London* brought to life.

This description seems impressionistic, subjective. Yet, if Waith is correct, our knowledge of Renaissance stage practice leads us to this picture. As Waith remarks, the beginning of the second act "[combines] a frank display of theatrical process with a kind of local color, since the setting up of the stage booths would, after all, approximate closely the setting up of the actual booths in the Fair."[7]

The single acting area does not limit the play, for Jonson's use of booths allows the audience's attention, as well as the characters', to be directed to a particular stage area at any given moment. The effect of this setting seems curiously modern; one is reminded of Peter Weiss's *Marat/Sade* or George Ryga's *The Ecstasy of Rita Joe,* plays in which a single stage set is used throughout while various areas within this main set suggest different locales in the world of the play.

The modern approach to collage staging is ultimately medieval; Waith points out that the setting for *Bartholomew Fair* is influenced by medieval traditions of staging, although he does not elaborate this point. For instance, *The Castle of Perseverance* has a setting very like that of *Bartholomew Fair,* for both plays use booths and simultaneous staging.[8] The difference in the mounting of the two plays is the placement of the audience. In *The Castle of Perseverance* the audience stood in the *platea,* at the center of the play, amidst the action taking place in and around the encircling mansions. In *Bartholomew Fair* the stage stands at the center of the action, and the audience surrounds the stage on three sides. This distinction suggests a major thematic difference between the two plays and between medieval and Renaissance drama. *The Castle of Perseverance* centered on its audience by acting out an allegorical presentation of each individual watching it. But *Bartholomew Fair* treats every member of its audience as either spectator or audience and suggests that the stage becomes the center for all human life.

By showing the fairground's public face and the disguised Adam Overdo's private thoughts, Jonson shows his audience the play's central tension: the difference between the true and assumed motives for an individual's actions. As Ray Heffner states it, "the central theme is the problem of what 'warrant' men have or pretend to have for their actions. . . . The emphasis in *Bartholomew Fair* is thus on the narrow range of motives that actually govern men's actions, in contrast to the wide variety of warrants they pretend to have."[9] The characters, save for poor Trouble-all, spend their time acting or watching others perform. The quarrel between

Trash and Leatherhead ends when the fairgoers appear; instead of arguing about the quality of each other's merchandise, they both call out to praise what they sell. Their "warrant" to be at the fair is the chance to make money, so private squabbling is forgotten for more agreeable public faces when customers come along. Throughout the rest of 2.2–3, the public and private faces of the fair are displayed as the play's focus shifts from the fair-at-large to Ursula's booth.

Overdo's mistakes as he listens to Ursula talk to Nightingale and Knockem are ironically funny because he mistakes private bantering for public enormity. The irony is underlined in 2.4 when he fails to hear the discussion of genuine enormity—prostitution and cutting purses—because he is preoccupied with his admiration for the civil cutpurse, Edgworth. Meanwhile, the fair-at-large continues: outside Ursula's booth in 2.4, the peddlers call to passers-by. (The repeated use of the "Cries of Smithfield" here and through the second and third acts suggests that Jonson expected this action to be effective.) The fair becomes more particularized in 2.4; in addition to hobbyhorses and gingerbread, fairgoers are offered mousetraps, flea tormentors, and relief for corns, while Nightingale not only offers ballads, but recites eight titles as well. This process of heaping up items continues throughout the play, as does the shift in focus between the fair-at-large and Ursula's booth. In the rest of act 2, for example, Trash and Leatherhead continue onstage, while first Winwife and Quarlous, then Cokes and his party are drawn into Ursula's booth. With both groups the violent side of the fair erupts. First Winwife and Quarlous argue with Ursula. She then goes into her booth and returns with the scalding pan to attack them; in the scuffle she falls and the hot liquid scalds her own leg. Next Cokes and his company enter. In 2.6 Cokes listens to Overdo rant, loses his purse, and rides piggyback on Wasp. This chain of events ends with the beating of Overdo when he is mistaken for the cutpurse. The action is fast and violent.

In the second act one thing is immediately noticeable about the appearance of the play on stage: the setting constantly changes. The changing appearance of the play suggests one of the chief paradoxes in the fair's nature. The fair is constant, yet protean. It remains before the audience and surrounds the characters in the play, but its landmarks keep changing as the focus shifts between the central booth and the smaller stands and as characters wander in and out. One moment it is filled with peddlers, the next with customers fighting, and then with an audience that watches a ballad singer. Yet the characters never show any difficulty in determining where in the fairground they are. The shifting landscape seems ordinary; the abnormal becomes normal.

In *Bartholomew Fair*, the shift in settings Jonson uses for *Volpone* is gone and he perfects the unified setting of *The Alchemist*. The audience need not even distinguish between the inside and outside of a house as they must in the fifth act of *The Alchemist*. Instead, all the action moves about a corner of the fairgrounds, and the characters set their own scenes. Because Jonson has contrived this kind of fluid setting for the fairground, the action seems very realistic. Yet beneath this realistic foreground, a sense of the magic nature of the fair remains. The fair springs up from nothing, Joan Trash sells gingerbread men who are her "progeny," Mooncalf is a "changeling" and an "incubee," and Nightingale sells

> "The Windmill blown down by the witch's fart!"
> Or "Saint George, that O! did break the dragon's heart!"
> (2.4.18–19)

In scene five, Ursula drops a pan of coals and becomes the goddess Discordia,[10] while Quarlous calls Lantern Leatherhead Orpheus, Joan Trash Ceres, and Jordan Knockem Neptune. From time to time throughout act 2, Leatherhead calls out to passersby, "What do you lack?" for whatever anyone lacks can be found somewhere in the booths of the fair. Jonson moves his play into the realm of the supernatural.

Act 2 ends with Overdo howling, "Murder, murder, murder!" As he runs away, the fair's customers follow him, leaving the stage to Trash and Leatherhead. When the watch enters at the start of act 3, Whit comments on their departure. "Nay, 'tish all gone, now!" he complains, and Bristle tells Haggis, "tou art in an oder 'orld . . . you met the man with the monsters, and I could not get you from him" (3.1.1, 3, 10–11). These speeches work in two ways: to evoke the real fairground where disturbances are not always quelled and freak shows distract even watchmen, and to suggest another world, a folk-tale world in which people vanish and monsters appear. The notion of magic is important, for in a magic world the normal causal connections disappear and with them disappears any reason to maintain a controlled outward appearance which grows from inner desire. The question of "warrant" is ultimately a question of causality, but in the shifting landscape of the fair normal cause-effect relationships are lost. One can become what one pleases or what others please. The roles one takes on have no connection to the rational.

In 3.2, twelvepence makes Quarlous into a Duke and Prince while the head man of the watch becomes a rogue and a pimp. Leatherhead peddles toys which transform children:

> What do you lack? What do you buy, pretty Mistress? a fine hobby-horse, to make your son a tilter? a drum to make a soldier? a fiddle to make him a reveller? What is't you lack? Little dogs for your daughters? or babies, male or female? (3.2.31–34)

But when the iconoclastic Busy speaks of the toys, they are transformed from talismans for an unborn child into lures for Satan:

> The wares are the wares of devils; and the whole Fair is the shop of Satan! They are hooks and baits, very baits, that are hung out on every side to catch you, and to hold you as it were, by the gills and by the nostrils, as the fisher doth; therefore, you must not look, nor turn toward them. The heathen man could stop his ears with wax against the harlot o' the sea; do you the like, with your fingers, against the bells of the Beast. (3.2.37–43)

Transformation follows transformation. In this speech, Busy first makes Satan into the fisher of men. Then he refers to Ulysses and the Sirens, but a few lines later the scent of the roast pig acts like Circe and turns him into a hound. Whit spouts doggerel like a romance hero and Knockem, the roarer, turns tapster.

One by one the characters disappear into Ursula's booth until the stage has only Trash, Leatherhead, Quarlous, and Winwife on it. In a scene parallel to 2.1, Overdo enters and launches into a soliloquy on the fair. In his first soliloquy he mistook the nature of the fair's enormities. In this parallel scene Overdo tries to make sense of events. His use of reason and reliance on causality are doomed from the outset. Like a figurative denial of any possibility for rational action, Cokes and his party enter as Overdo leaves.

Unlike Overdo, Cokes is completely comfortable at the fair. He has no trouble regarding fiction as reality, for he thinks toy violins are suitable for real musicians, mistakes a ballad's characters for historical personages, and changes his roles as quickly as he turns around. One moment he is Wasp's student, the next a would-be father, then landlord, bridegroom, host, audience, thief taker, and victim. His props create his roles. As Cokes bargains with Lantern Leatherhead and Joan Trash for their wares, Quarlous asks, "Are you removing the Fair?" (3.4.61). Quarlous's facetiousness is ironic, for Cokes would indeed like to take the whole fair home with him. Yet he cannot, for the fair is more than an armload of toys; it is people too, and, as 3.4 makes clear, people cannot be bought.[11] Wasp, furious at Cokes's purchases, attacks Leatherhead:

> *Wasp.*   Cry you mercy! you'd be sold too, would you? What's the price on you? Jerkin and all, as you stand? Ha' you any qualities?
> *Trash.*   Yes, goodman angry-man, you shall find he has qualities, if you cheapen him.
> *Wasp.*   Godso, you ha' the selling of him! What are they? Will they be bought for love or money?
> *Trash.*   No indeed, sir.
>
> (3.4.102–9)

Joan Trash's reply is a good one; the fair is a place of total freedom, so that people cannot be bought or sold against their will. Later Whit tries to buy Win and Mistress Overdo; the attempt fails when Mistress Overdo vomits and reveals herself. Again, Purecraft seeks to buy a madman for her husband and Overdo tries to buy Grace for Cokes. But Quarlous is far from mad and cheats Purecraft, while Grace follows a madman's advice and escapes Cokes. Toys can be sold; people cannot.

Overdo is lost in the fair because of his rationality. Cokes is completely at home until his purse is stolen and he can buy no more. Then he follows Wasp once again, helping him haul away the unfortunate Overdo to the watch. Although Cokes has a better understanding of the fair's nature than Overdo has, he is a poor spectator. Spectators must accept a performance on the performer's terms, without trying, as Overdo does, to impose a different set of values on an artificial creation. But spectators must also watch every aspect of a performance. Those who are too entranced by one aspect, such as a ballad, are apt to overlook a more important aspect, such as a cutpurse. Of course, these ideas recall the Induction. In the contract Jonson tells his audience not to judge his play by the wrong set of standards. It is not set in "the sword-and-buckler age of Smithfield," it is not *Jeronimo or Andronicus*," nor is it one of the "Tales, Tempests, and such like drolleries." Moreover, his audience should not pick out one part of the play and ignore the rest. *Bartholomew Fair* is not an allegory or a satire on individuals; it is not a play of scurrility or profaneness.

As if to underline both points, act 3 ends with Rabbi Busy's assault on the fair. Not only does he try to fit the fairground into the framework of Puritan theology; he concentrates on toys and gingerbread while ignoring the fair's real sins. Busy's attack on idolatry begins with his complaints against Ursula:

> Urs'la is above all to be avoided, having the marks upon her of the three enemies of man: the world, as being in the Fair; the devil, as being in the fire; and the flesh, as being herself. (3.6.33–35)

But he fails to notice that she represents the world, the devil, and the flesh by harboring thieves, by encouraging violence and gluttony, and by procuring prostitutes. When Busy turns his attention to Trash and Leatherhead's stands, he neglects this greater menace to righteousness in Ursula's booth, which looms at the back of the stage. Lest we miss the point, Jonson brings Busy's fulmination to a climax with the wonderful lines:

> See you not Goldylocks, the purple strumpet, there, in her yellow gown and green sleeves? the profane pipes, the tinkling timbrels? A shop of relics! (3.6.86–88)

As he pulls over the gingerbread stand, the audience laughs at his ignorance. The real strumpets are in Ursula's booth and the only "profane pipes" or "tinkling timbrels" in the fair are Nightingale's ballads that mask thievery. The act concludes with Busy's arrest; like Overdo, the Puritan is a foolish spectator.

Overdo, Cokes, and Busy are all punished in the fourth act. Yet Overdo's and Busy's punishments are less severe than they might be, thanks to the madman Trouble-all, who also provides Cokes with a rare opportunity to feel superior. The act begins and ends by focusing on the stocks; the second and third scenes are set in an unlocalized area of the fairgrounds; the fourth and fifth take place in front of Ursula's booth. The shifts in focus which began in act 2 proliferate as the plot complications grow and as each character's wish takes him farther away from his normal world.

Overdo is in the stocks because he wants to track down wickedness. Busy, too, is brought to the stocks far from his Banbury congregation because he seeks out wickedness. Later in the act Wasp, the play's third authority figure, is brought to the stocks as well. As authority figures, all three should be good men who watch over others. In *Discoveries*, Jonson speaks of good men and their role in the world:

. . . they, plac'd high on top of all vertue, look'd downe on the Stage of the world, and contemned the Play of *Fortune*. For though the most be Players, some must be Spectators.[12]

Clearly Overdo, Busy, and Wasp fail. Not only are they poor spectators when they judge the fair, they are also active participants in the fair. Yet spectators give a kind of static performance; they exist to be observed. Jonson insists that *"Good men* are the Stars, the Planets of the Ages wherein they live, and illustrate the times."[13] None of these three serves as a good example when the public looks to them for authority. Wasp, in act 5, finds his authority over Cokes completely gone. Busy behaves hypocritically throughout the play and particularly during the puppet show. Overdo, who is at least well-intentioned, behaves irresponsibly nevertheless. First he abandons Pie Powders court for the day, leaving the entire fair without authority. (One notes the watch's confusion over what to do with the prisoners.) Moreover, he is and has been harsh and inaccurate in his judgment. The audience has watched him make error after error, mistaking Edgworth for a virtuous young man, worrying about watered ale while overlooking prostitution. The appearance of Trouble-all with his obsession about "warrant" suggests Overdo's past harshness and mistaking. Yet Trouble-all's appearance also saves Overdo from the stocks. In 4.1 the watch are made uneasy by Trouble-all's insistence on warrant and carry Overdo and Busy to Pie Powders court. In 4.6 they are annoyed by him again and in the ensuing confusion their prisoners escape. Overdo's failing brings him a kind of mad mercy.

Leatherhead's call in acts 2 and 3 of "What do you lack?" is replaced in act 4 by Trouble-all's more difficult question "Have you a warrant?" Though the fair offers all the characters the answers to their wishes, it also calls into question their motivation in coming to the fairgrounds. The greediest of the fairgoers is Cokes, who wants nothing less than the whole of the fair. His greed for the sights and sounds of the fair has cost him two purses; in 4.2 it leads him to scramble for pears and lose his clothes as well. When Trouble-all appears Cokes says hopefully, "Pray thee guide me to [my] house." But Trouble-all insists on Overdo's warrant and leaves Cokes to wander through the fairgrounds. In this scene, Cokes's inanity results in his feeling superior to Trouble-all. Moreover, it leads him, finally, to the puppet show, which delights him. Again a character's failing is rewarded.

In the Grace-Winwife-Quarlous subplot, Trouble-all functions as a *deus ex machina,* popping in and out at convenient moments. All three characters have the same wish—to find a spouse—and all three dissemble to attain their end. Yet when they trust their fates to a madman, they are not punished but rewarded. Winwife and Grace escape unattractive marriages by winning each other, while Quarlous wins a rich widow and "warrant" for his wedding from Justice Overdo.

Within the play, Trouble-all asks the most difficult question, but those who face it, though they fail to understand it, are treated with mercy, even rewarded. The question of warrant is carried out on stage by a pattern of presentational imagery. As in *Volpone,* a great many pieces of paper are handed about on stage—the play begins with Littlewit holding Cokes's wedding license, Adam Overdo carries about a black book in which he writes down all the enormities of the fair, Nightingale hawks ballad sheets, Grace makes her choice of husband from the names written in a pair of tables, Overdo writes out his warrant for the disguised Quarlous, and the puppet show is described on the bill which Cokes reads. But all of the pieces of paper appear false; like the props in *The Alchemist,* they are not used for their intended purposes. Overdo's black book lists all of the enormities he thinks he sees—all the times those about him act without legal warrant—yet he is mistaken in his observations, misled by appearance. Nightingale's ballad sheets are his warrant for being at the fair, where he and Edgworth do their real work as cutpurses. A madman's random choice becomes Grace's warrant for marrying Winwife, while Overdo's warrant is mistakenly given to Quarlous instead of to Trouble-all. The papers serve as excuses for warrant, but there is no real warrant at *Bartholomew Fair.* Nor can there be: the authority figures have abdicated their responsibilities in order to gawk and to perform at the fair.

The falsity of the written language is matched by the false speech of the vapors scene (4.4) and the seduction scene (4.5), both set at Ursula's booth. In these scenes the fairgrounds' inhabitants tell the fairgoers enormous lies, largely for the sheer pleasure of using language. Win and Mistress Overdo are essentially ignorant about, though compliant with, Whit's and Knockem's proposal, yet the two men vie with each other in hyperbole, topping lie with lie. They spin, as Knockem says, "Brave vapors!" for the two women. In contrast to their brave vapors, Ramping Alice's "Catamountain vapors" recall the game of 4.4 "which is nonsense: every man to oppose the last that spoke, whether it concerned him or no"

(4.4.29, stage direction). In the game of vapors, a drunken flood of contradiction and qualification washes away all meaning. All of the fair's innate violence emerges here as everyone fights, yet the violence too is false. No one is hurt by the insults or the drunken blows. On the contrary, they enjoy themselves, and when the watch arrive to arrest Wasp, he asks them plaintively, "Cannot a man quarrel in quietness . . . ?" (4.4.157–58). By the end of act 4 a pattern emerges. In the mutable world of the fair, nothing is what it appears to be. The spectators on the stage and in the audience must watch carefully or they will be taken in by Bartholomew Fair.

As the characters wander from booth to booth, each one's wish comes true, although no one gets what he intended. The Littlewits have a good time, but not together. John eats his fill, sees his fill, and finds his puppet play put on to great applause—but he loses his wife. Win falls in with Whit, who persuades her to abandon the restraints of marriage as well as those of Puritanism; she puts on a green gown and becomes a prostitute. Like Win, Mistress Overdo is recruited as a prostitute without realizing it; still, she manages to keep all around her serene until she finds her husband, who is appalled to see her. Purecraft finds her gentlemanly madman, Winwife and Quarlous see the sport and win wives, and Grace finds a new husband to free her from her engagement to Cokes. However, Purecraft's "madman" is only pretending madness; Quarlous's wife is wealthy, but the sort of wife he warned his friend against in act 1; and Winwife's Grace has a fortune which may be forfeit by her marriage. Cokes manages to buy up most of the fair, making it his in fact as well as name, only to lose it all. Wasp finds the game of vapors and all the quarrelling he could desire, but he ends up arrested and loses all control over Cokes. Rabbi Busy eats and prophesies exceedingly until he confesses publicly he is a hypocrite. And Adam Overdo does finally learn the truth about the fair, but at the cost of learning the truth about himself.

No one who comes into the fair is happy with what he has, and the fair provides each with something new. But the characters remain dissatisfied even after their wishes have been fulfilled. The suspension of the normal order of the world combines with the constant questioning—What do you lack? What is your warrant?—to lead the characters to self-knowledge by play's end. Not even this self-knowledge is completely free from discord: while Justice Overdo and the others begin to understand what has happened to them at the fair, full understanding must wait until they have left the fairgrounds for a dinner at Overdo's house.

This dinner is a comic convention, a feast of reconciliation, yet it also serves as part of a pattern of eating and drinking in the play. Jonson calls for props of ale, gingerbread, pears, and roast pig during the play. Most, though not all, of the action involving food occurs when characters enter the fair and try to satisfy their appetites at Ursula's booth. The fair is a place to satisfy the appetite but its central booth houses discord; characters taste the fair's food and their adventures begin. The nature of the fair is paradoxical and magical.

But the effect of its nature on the characters is to force them to recognize reality. Intangibles are worthless at Smithfield; morality and integrity count for nothing, and the normal system of punishment is nonexistent. One must simply have the appearance of warrant for what one does, and even warrant itself must be made tangible by the pieces of paper used throughout. The world of *Bartholomew Fair* has become completely reified, and the reification is emphasized by the diversity of *things* which appear on stage and among the booths. Even a partial list of props for the play is a hodgepodge: it includes gingerbread men, hobbyhorses, tinderboxes, corncutters, pipes, toy birds, drums, swords, ale mugs, a basket of puppets, all the pieces of false paper.

The only accurate piece of paper is the puppets' bill, and only the puppets can be said to have warrant for what they do. The bill reads "The ancient modern history of *Hero and Leander*, otherwise called *The Touchstone of True Love*, with as true a trial of friendship between Damon and Pythias, two faithful friends o' the Bankside" (5.3.6–9), and this is exactly what the play offers. It is both ancient and modern since it is a contemporary reworking of classical stories. Moreover, it combines Marlowe's *Hero and Leander* with Richard Edwards' *Damon and Pythias*.[14] When Busy challenges the puppets' warrant for performing, Leatherhead assures him, "I have the Master of the Revel's hand for it, sir" (5.5.18). Yet the puppets, like the fair, are false in appearance, action, and language. Theirs is a completely fictive world in which wooden dolls pretend to be men, fighting, wooing, and drinking like the people in the fair. The lines they speak are the worst sort of poetry, jangling doggerel in which cant, vulgarity, and nonsense predominate. Their acting breaks all conventions as they step in and out of character or beat Leatherhead. Still they take in the ninny Cokes and the hypocrite Busy. Leatherhead must assure Cokes, "Between you and I, sir, we do but make show" (5.4.253).

Busy attacks the morality of the performance, but to no avail.

Each time he makes a charge, the puppet Dionysius denies it with a quibble. When Busy finally complains that actors are transvestites, he forgets the essential falsity of the puppets' appearance, and Dionysius confutes him by proving that "we have neither male nor female amongst us" (5.5.92–93). The puppet play, like all the paper, mocks those at the fair who are taken in by appearance, yet the mockery is good-humored. No one suffers because he has been taken in, no one loses by his mistakes, unlike the characters in *Volpone*, *Epicoene*, or *The Alchemist*. Everyone remains free to go home, leaving the booths of the fair behind for another year.

The final scenes of *Bartholomew Fair* mirror the real situation of its performance. As the audiences at the Hope and at court watched the Lady Elizabeth's Men, so the actors watch the puppets. The reflection is not flattering to the real audience, for the puppets' audience is made up of bigots, fools, and bawds. Cokes cannot even distinguish between puppets and real men; Rabbi Zeal-of-the-Land Busy not only fails to distinguish between them; he is defeated in his argument with a puppet.

Yet one might ask if the mirror is really so unflattering. The greatest fool on stage, Cokes, cannot tell the difference between the wooden actors and the human audience. If the audience in the theater confuses itself with the audience of actors onstage, it makes the same error. In the play's Induction, Jonson had warned against that very sort of identification when he cautioned *"politic pick-locks"* not to confuse real people with the characters onstage. Instead of seeing himself in the play, everyone in Jonson's audience is invited to join those actor-spectators in laughter. The butt of that laughter is anyone who cannot distinguish actors and spectators.

In the final scenes of the play, Jonson's view of his audience is not a bitter one. He laughs at those who foolishly confuse the world and the stage, but also reminds the spectators that world and stage cannot be wholly separated. Adam Overdo must recognize that he was not the only actor in the world of the play and that what he thought reality was in fact acting. To know that men are both actors and spectators within the theater or out of it, yet never to confuse one's own role-playing with reality—this is the attitude Jonson seeks. His comments in *Discoveries* on *theatrum mundi* have special relevance:

*I have* considered, our whole life is like a *Play:* wherein every man, forgetfull of himselfe, is in travaile with expression of another. Nay, wee so insist in imitating others, as wee cannot (when it is necessary) returne to our selves: like Children, that imitate the vices of *Stammer-ers* so long, till at last they become such; and make the habit to another nature, as it is never forgotten.[15]

Overdo's attitude is wrong, and when he realizes his mistake, he says to all, "I invite you home with me to my house, to supper. I will have none fear to go along, for my intents are *ad correctionem, non ad destructionem; ad aedificandum, non ad diruendum.* So lead on" (5.6.107–9). He will learn to distinguish between the actor and the real man within himself. But Cokes's final line is equally pertinent: "we'll ha' the rest o' the play at home" (5.6.110). The play goes on, within the theater or within the world outside the playhouse.

## [ 3 ]

# The Play's Influence: 1614–1660

THE history of *Bartholomew Fair*'s first performances suggests its family ties to the Smithfield fair. The fair began because of royal patronage, thrived because of its spectators, and survived despite religious dissension. Jonson shaped his play for two kinds of spectators—commoners and royalty—and focused his play on the role of spectator. But the satire on the Puritans made the play controversial; religious dissension meant that *Bartholomew Fair* nearly died in the troubled years from 1614 to 1660.

No one knows how well the audience at the Hope or at court liked *Bartholomew Fair*. Generally, modern scholars think that the play was well received, but not as successful as *Volpone, Epicoene,* or *The Alchemist,* which were highly praised and often revived.[1] An eighteenth-century tradition, recorded by William Oldys, says that Jonson's contemporaries so loved *Bartholomew Fair* that it drew the praise, "O, rare Ben Jonson," but this tradition, though attractive, is untrustworthy.[2] No solid evidence exists about the play's popularity before the Restoration.

Facts about the first fifty years of *Bartholomew Fair*'s life are hard to come by. I would like to sketch a possible history for the play, then to examine that history in detail. The public and court audiences enjoyed the play, and it was probably revived in Jonson's lifetime. The allusions to it during the period from 1614 to 1660 argue for the play's popularity and public familiarity with the work. If it was not revived in full, part of it may have been performed illegally as an anti-Puritan satire during the Commonwealth. Such a revival would help to account for the play's early return to the London stage after Charles II was restored to the throne and for the surge of popularity it enjoyed through the first part of the eighteenth century.

But despite the play's initial success, at the Hope and at court, it failed to satisfy its author. At the height of his career, Jonson held it back from his ground-breaking 1616 Folio, not abandoning it, but hoping to rework it into a better play. What he had done in *Bartholomew Fair* was central to his critical credo, and he planned to use the play as an exemplar of his own work in his discussion of Horace's *Ars Poetica*. Finally, ill health and financial necessity forced him to try to publish *Bartholomew Fair*, but his bad luck continued in his choice of a printer, for the man he picked was incompetent. Literary integrity proved greater than his need for money, and he gave up the project. Ironically, because he refused to go on with it, the only text extant is the one he refused to sanction.

When one examines the influence that the play had on other Jacobean and Caroline playwrights, on pamphlets, and on Jonson's own work, one realizes that the work was well-known in its own day. In part, of course, the work was well-known because Jonson was known. During the seventeenth century, Jonson's reputation reached its zenith; many, perhaps most, readers considered him the greatest of all British playwrights, not excluding Shakespeare.[3] But Jonson's reputation was hardly the only reason, nor even the major reason, for the success that the play had: not only did its topical satire attract attention, but the audience also remembered and laughed at the play's grotesque characters. Other playwrights were struck by incidents in the play and its use of setting. The extent of this influence strongly suggests that the play was revived, although no records of such revivals exist any longer.

Scholars have pointed out that at least four of Jonson's contemporaries wrote plays that seem to borrow incidents from *Bartholomew Fair*: these dramatists are Richard Brome, Thomas Middleton, Robert Ward, and James Shirley; moreover, the play may have been the model for later topographical comedies.[4] Only in the case of Brome is the borrowing explicit, but one cannot overlook the other dramatists, even if the "influence" of *Bartholomew Fair* seems illusory.

Richard Brome refers most directly to Jonson's play, a fact that is hardly surprising since he worked on the original production. One might assume that his play *The Weeding of Covent Garden* (1632) shows nothing about the initial success or continuing popularity of *Bartholomew Fair* and a great deal about Brome's close relationship to his former master Jonson. Nonetheless, Brome did expect his audience to understand the following speech by Cockbrain:

> And so, as my Reverend Ancestor, *Justice Adam Overdoe*, was wont to say, *In Heavens name and the Kings*, and for the good of the Common-wealth, I will go about it." (1.1)[5]

Unless *Bartholomew Fair* had enjoyed some popularity, the spectators would miss the point of the joke here. Moreover, the play's plot and some of its characters are reminiscent of *Bartholomew Fair*.[6] Since Brome uses Cockbrain's speech explicitly to call the audience's attention to the debt he owes Jonson, one might assume he expected his audience to notice the *extent* of his debt throughout the rest of the play as well.

Middleton is another dramatist who may be in debt to Jonson and his play. Two of Middleton's plays are said to show the influence of *Bartholomew Fair: The Widow* (1616) and *The Mayor of Queenborough, or Hengist, King of Kent* (1615–1620).[7] At one point, scholars thought Jonson had co-authored *The Widow* since his name and John Fletcher's appear on the play's title page, but now scholars agree that neither Jonson nor Fletcher had a hand in it.[8] The mistaken attribution of authorship does suggest the Jonsonian elements in *The Widow*. In both *Bartholomew Fair* and *The Widow*, cutpurses (Edgworth, Latrocinio) ply their trade on stage; in both plays a justice (Overdo, Brandino) gives a seal to a disguised rascal (Quarlous, Latrocinio) who uses it to forge a legal document. (Other Jonson plays on which Middleton may draw in *The Widow* are *Epicoene, The Alchemist, Volpone,* and *The Devil Is an Ass*.)[9] Another of Middleton's plays, *The Mayor of Queenborough, or Hengist, King of Kent,* seems to make use of Busy's debate with the puppets. In act 5 the mayor, Simon, forces his political rival, the Puritan Oliver, to watch a play. Like Busy, Oliver is outraged, but he soon lapses into sullen discomfiture. Instead it is Simon who behaves like Busy by actually talking to the performers and entering into the play—where he has his pocket picked as does Cokes in *Bartholomew Fair*.[10]

Like Middleton, Robert Ward may have been drawn to the scene of Busy's fight with the puppets when he wrote the Latin comedy, *Fucus Histriomastix* (1623).[11] The character Fucus is a hypocritical Puritan who argues against academic drama. This circumstance by itself would not demonstrate that *Bartholomew Fair* was a source for Ward's play, of course, but there are a number of other similarities. Fucus is not only a Puritan, but also a short-tempered tutor like Wasp. Moreover, at one point in the play Fucus has a character put in the stocks; most of the fourth act of *Bartholomew Fair* is taken up with a similar line of plot. None of these similarities is decisive, and in this case, the influence of *Bartholomew Fair* must be viewed as "not proven." Certainly Ward *could* have known Jonson's play. Since Ward had just received his B.A. in 1615, he might have seen Jonson's play when it was first performed, though he would be more likely to have known of it from a later performance.[12]

There is another important similarity between *Fucus Histriomastix* and *Bartholomew Fair,* but it is a coincidence growing out of the plays' first performances. Like Jonson's play, Ward's *Fucus Histriomastix* had two opening nights. It was first given at Queen's College, Cambridge, despite a certain amount of religious controversy, and then performed with another Latin play, *Loiola.* Attempts were made to block *Loiola*'s production:

> . . . the king meant to have been [at Cambridge] this Shrovetide, to see certain plays, about which there hath been much ado 'twixt the master and seniors of Trinity College on the one side, and the younger fellows on the other, who would have them by all means; so that, the matter being referred to the vice-chancellor, he loth to displease either party, sent it to the lord keeper, who acquainting the king with it, certain of both parties were sent for, about Christmas, to show their reasons, which, not being admitted on the seniors' side, but willed to bring better or more pregnant, the ancientest of them said, that these times required rather prayers and fasting than plays and feasting: which was ill taken, and order given for the plays to go on.[13]

And go on they did. *Loiola* and *Fucus Histriomastix* were performed for the University in the spring of 1622–23. Another performance of Ward's play was probably given the next month before King James, who had helped get it produced in the first place.[14] Thus the play was performed both for a public audience and for the King. As when he watched *Bartholomew Fair,* James watched a Puritan, who attacked the theater, put firmly down.

The figure of the bad-tempered tutor attracted James Shirley as well as Robert Ward. But the character of Wasp is like two characters in Shirley's *The Witty Fair One* (1628): the discontented Tutor who shepherds about the Cokes-like Sir Nicholas Treedle, and the

contentious Brains who chaperones Violetta.[15] One of the funniest
scenes of the play occurs when the two get together. The Tutor
attacks Brains, and Brains beats off the Tutor; in revenge, the Tutor
has Brains arrested (though, unlike Wasp, Brains is not put in the
stocks). Like Grace Wellborn, Violetta in Shirley's play is intended
for a ninny, Treedle, but she manages to avoid her wedding by
eloping with Aimwell when she goes to buy a trousseau. Not
knowing what her plans are, Treedle gives her money and sends
her off on her shopping expedition, declaring:

> Violetta, look you lay out my gold at the Exchange in Bartholomew-
> fairings; farewell, Violetta. (4.2.115–17)

She goes to buy "Bartholomew-fairings" and returns as another
man's wife. Certainly this speech seems to allude directly to Grace
in Jonson's play.

All five of these plays—*The Weeding of Covent Garden*, *The
Widow*, *The Mayor of Queenborough, or Hengist, King of Kent*,
*Fucus Histriomastix*, and *The Witty Fair One*—may draw on Jonson's play. If this influence exists, then Jonson's play continued to
be remembered by London playwrights from 1616, only two years
after its first production, until 1632, nearly twenty years later.
Such an influence would suggest that the play was successful in its
original productions, that it remained popular, and that it was
revived, although no record remains to show that such revivals
took place.

Another item that may indicate the success of the 1614 productions is a pamphlet, "Bartholomew Faire or Variety of fancies
where you may find a faire of wares, and all to please your mind"
(1641).[16] Without question, the pamphlet draws on Jonson's play
to describe people who attend Smithfield fair. It begins by listing
the wide variety of fairgoers:

> Hither resort people of all sorts, High and Low, Rich and Poore, from
> cities, townes, and countrys; of all sects, Papists, Atheists, Anabap-
> tists, and Brownists: and of all conditions, good and bad, vertuous and
> vitious, Knaves and fooles, Cuckolds and Cuckoldmakers, Bauds, and
> Whores, Pimpes and Panders, Rogues and Rascalls, the little Loud-one
> and the witty Wanton. (P. 167)

Yet the rest of the pamphlet concentrates only on specific characters modelled on those found in Jonson's play. It describes a pig-
stall kept by a "fat greasy Hostesse" like Ursula who cheats a

pregnant woman longing for a pig's head. At another point, the pamphlet tells of a fairgoer who loses hat and cloak when he puts them down in order to gather some pears that have been dropped; this stratagem is the same one Jonson uses in 4.2 of *Bartholomew Fair*. A description of an angry Puritan who attacks the fair recalls Rabbi Busy's speeches against it in 3.6:

> . . . he begins in a violent passion, to exclaime against the Idolatry of the times, that it was growne abominable; protesting that the whore of *Babilon* was crept into Christ Church, and that the good motions of the Spirit had brought him to towne, to make a sacrifice of those Idle Idolls, to his just anger and holy indignation. . . . (P. 168)

Busy is a hypocrite, while the Puritan of the pamphlet seems to be sincere; nonetheless, they both speak of the same things in the same way.

The pamphlet's use of Jonson's play might suggest that the author had seen the play more recently than 1614 or had heard about it from others who had seen and enjoyed performances. At first it seems to show that Jonson's play had enjoyed a fair amount of success, enough to have had its plots and characters pass into the popular imagination by 1641, twenty-seven years after the only known productions. However, the play had its first publication in the second volume of Jonson's folio *Works* which appeared in 1641–42.[17] A similar case occurs with regard to an allusion to Busy in Richard Brathwaite's *Whimzies* (1631).[18] Jonson's abortive edition of three comedies, including *Bartholomew Fair*, was printed, but not distributed, in 1631. Thus Brathwaite could have known about Busy's antics either from seeing them on stage or from a privately circulated copy of *Bartholomew Fair*. (I discuss the 1631 edition in more detail below.) In short, the pamphlets may possibly draw on the published versions of the play, rather than on successful stage revivals of *Bartholomew Fair*.

The year following the play's publication saw the beginning of the Puritan commonwealth. In 1642, at the start of the Civil War, Parliament, which the Puritans dominated, issued orders to close all theaters for five years. At the end of this trial prohibition period, entrepreneurs made plans to reopen the theaters, but in vain. The theaters remained closed until the Restoration.[19] Even had they been open, a play which attacked Puritan hypocrisy as enthusiastically as *Bartholomew Fair* would not have been welcomed. In her recent book, *Puritanism and Theatre*, Margot Heinemann argues that Jonson was the playwright least liked by the Puritans, though he was not, of course, the only one to attack them.[20] Thus in the anonymous Puritan pamphlet, *The non-such Charles his character*, the Puritan author uses a fictionalized account of Jonson's death to illustrate what happens to anyone who trusts in kings—sordid poverty and ingratitude.[21] As long as the Puritans were in power, neither Jonson nor Rabbi Busy was welcome in London.

While Jonson's plays were not legally performed between 1642 and 1660, operas and public play readings did occur, as well as illegal private performances of plays.[22] (Illegal bear-baiting also took place—and at the Hope. In September 1655, one of the Hope's bears killed a child; the next year the Hope was shut up with some finality: bears were shot and mastiffs shipped to Jamaica.)[23] Actors continued to find work at the Red Bull Theatre, though it was dangerous employment since they were sometimes arrested.[24] Holland House, a nobleman's home, was another spot where unsanctioned performances took place.[25] One interesting development was that the illegal performances were often drolls, that is, short sketches, often scenes adapted from full-length plays, rather than the play itself. A droll based on part of *Bartholomew Fair* would have met with success from an audience which disliked the Puritan regime, especially its edict against playgoing.

The anonymous work, "A Bartholomew Fairing, New, New, New: Sent from the Raised Siege before *Dublin*, as a Preparatory Present to the Great Thanksgiving Day" (1649), is not a droll.[26] Instead, "A Bartholomew Fairing" is a political pamphlet in the form of a short play that draws on Jonson's work—if only for its title. Quite aside from the title, the pamphlet's characters, all Puritans, employ Busy's rhetorical tricks of repetition and amplification.[27] In 1.6 of *Bartholomew Fair*, Busy announces, ". . . I will go and eat. I will eat exceedingly and prophesy. . . . I will therefore eat, yea, I will eat exceedingly," and the scene ends with his line, "Very likely, exceedingly likely, very exceedingly likely." In "A Bartholomew Fairing" Mrs. Tryall sounds like Busy: ". . . this gift of New Park, in sooth sister was it not a pat, a very pat and opposite, a very pertinent, and as Mr. Goodwine said, a very sutable and agreeing Present for us . . ." (pp. 1–2). Not only does she repeat and amplify pointlessly, she also uses the intensive "very" as Busy does, though she ignores his pet word "exceedingly." In 2.6 of Jonson's play, Overdo has a tirade against tobacco, which associates the "tawny weed" with its New World origins. Overdo's lecture may have inspired Ralph's speech in praise of tobacco in "A Bartholomew Fairing":

> Sir, I have a piece of singular Tobacco for your Muse. The very prime of the leaf. *Ochechampano Poca-Hunto*'s Father great *Custos* of the Indies drinks not so good. (P. 6)

There may be another slight allusion to *Bartholomew Fair* in Mr. Lerned's confession, "I am a *Hinde* at prose, but a dull Ox / At verse, *my feet* are as they'd been ith' stocks," (p. 6). The most direct reference, however, is Lerned's advice to Ralph to " . . . drink no Clarret to night, that will furre the throat, let *Ursula* make you some butter'd ale . . ." (p. 6). The pamphlet against the Puritans draws on Jonson's play, which suggests that *Bartholomew Fair*, whether it was revived or not, was recognized by the anti-Puritanical author as a source for arguments against and mockery of Cromwell and his supporters. In short, while Jonson's play is only known to have been performed in 1614, it still had some influence in 1649.

After the Restoration, *Bartholomew Fair* was quickly revived. Sir Henry Herbert included *Bartholomew Fair* in a 1661 list of plays acted by the King's Company.[28] Since the play was the second of Jonson's plays revived, it might seem that the London public remembered and had enjoyed productions of *Bartholomew Fair*. Because the popularity of a pair of performances in 1614 would hardly last almost fifty years, this would suggest that the play had been revived either before the Puritan rule or illegally during the Commonwealth. However, the play might have been remembered because of its published version in 1640–41 or even revived because of its attack on the Puritans. This latter alternative seems unlikely, though, since the attack on the Puritans was toned down during the early years of the Restoration. Jonson's satire was muted in the first two Restoration productions, which omitted the confrontation between the puppets and the Puritan Rabbi Busy.[29] In 1661 Pepys remarked on the third Restoration production, one which did include the puppets:

> September 7th. . . . And here was *Bartholomew fayre*, with the Puppet-Shewe, acted today, which had not been these forty years (it being so satyricall against puritanisme, they durst not till now; which is strange they should already dare to do it, and the King to countenance it)[30]

Pepys's comments make it clear that *Bartholomew Fair* was not revived, at least initially, in a fit of gloating over the Puritans; it was revived because it was popular. Only after it had succeeded without the satire did the actors perform it with the satire that so shocked Pepys. (Later Restoration audiences did use the play to gloat, as I will explain in Chapter 4.)

These bits of evidence suggest success, but the suggestion is a tenuous one, founded on implication and inference. Aside from the evidence of the play's influence, there are no contemporary references to productions of the play, nor are there records of revivals. This lack of contemporary references and records does not mean that they never existed. Perhaps the play was often revived and discussed, but these references have disappeared over the intervening centuries, as so many data about the Renaissance theater have. In a way, however, this silence is, in itself, a hint that the play enjoyed success and further productions. Ben Jonson was a controversial figure all his life. When a play of his failed completely, his contemporaries commented on it, while he commented on his contemporaries and their bad taste. No Jonsonian comment assails the actors or audiences of *Bartholomew Fair,* and Jonson never suffered quietly when his work was attacked.

Although Jonson never commented on the stage productions of his play, he did comment on his own work in the play. After Jonson's visit in 1619, the Scots poet William Drummond wrote:

> To me he read the Preface of his arte of Poesie, upon Horace Arte of Poesie, wher he heth ane apologie of a Play of his St Bartholomee's faire, by Criticus is understood Done.[31]

One wonders what happened to Jonson's apology for his play, what *Bartholomew Fair* has to do with Horace, and how Donne became a character in such an apology. This is a tantalizing piece of literary gossip. Jonson's poem, "An Execration upon Vulcan" mourns the loss of the Horatian translations in a 1623 fire; presumably his apology for the play perished with them.[32] Yet two different translations of the *Ars Poetica* done by Jonson *were* published, one in the 1640 Duodecimo edition, the other in the 1640 Folio.[33] Although they were both published *after* Jonson's fire—and after his death—they were written well before 1623. Perhaps Jonson's friends had copies of his translations to replace the loss; it seems strange that no copy of the apology, with its remarks to or about John Donne, survived.

George Burke Johnston has advanced an attractive theory to account for the loss of Jonson's apology while some of his other works were rewritten. If Jonson were a professor of rhetoric at Gresham College, the works that he rewrote might be those he needed for his teaching.[34] The other works were not required for the classroom and hence were never rewritten. Certainly as a professor of rhetoric, Jonson would have used Horace in his lectures, while the apology for *Bartholomew Fair*, appended to his translation of Horace, would not have been needed.

The question remains why the apology was written at all. Why did Jonson feel the need for a formal justification or defense of his work in *Bartholomew Fair*? He may have been responding to adverse criticism (which has disappeared) or reconciling his work with the Horatian dicta of the *Ars Poetica*. In any case, if Jonson felt it necessary to write an apology, he was evidently dissatisfied with some critical matter connected with the play.

Some such dissatisfaction may have been inevitable, given Jonson's strong personal ties with the play and its production. To begin with, Jonson frequently revised his plays after they had been performed. In the case of *Bartholomew Fair* he had grown up knowing of the fair and may have been a puppeteer there; some of his close friends worked in the first production of his play. Given these circumstances, a perfectionist like Jonson was unlikely to feel completely happy with his play, wanting it to be better than it was.

*Bartholomew Fair*'s curious publishing history supports the hypothesis that Jonson was dissatisfied. The play was performed in 1614, but two years later, when Jonson published his Folio *Works*, he chose *not* to include *Bartholomew Fair* in this collection. Although it was the last play he wrote before publishing the 1616 Folio, he produced two masques, *The Golden Age Restored* and *Mercury Vindicated from the Alchemists at Court*, after *Bartholomew Fair* and included both in the 1616 Folio.[35] Of course if the play still held the stage in 1616, two years after its first production, he would have had an excellent reason for leaving it unpublished—to deny other companies access to a popular text. A masque, on the other hand, posed no threat to the company since it could only be produced—expensively—at court.

Ben Jonson did not consider *Bartholomew Fair* suitable for inclusion in an edition of collected works. One cannot say, however, that Jonson disliked or repudiated *Bartholomew Fair*. He was enough in earnest about the play to write an apology to it and to include that apology as part of the work he did on his much-loved Horace. In addition, Jonson mentions the play in his poem "An Expostulation with Inigo Jones" (1631?), as an example of how amusing silly actions can be. Angered by Jones, Jonson first attacks him, then relents a bit and writes:

> I am too fat t'enuy him. He too leane,
> To be worth Enuy. Henceforth I doe meane
> To pitty him, as smiling at his feat
> Of Lanterne-lerry: wth fuliginous heat
> Whirling his Whymseys, by a subtilty
> Suckt from ye Veynes of shop-philosophy.
> What would he doe now, gi'ng his mynde yt waye
> In presentaĉon of some puppet play!
> Should but ye king his Iustice-hood employ
> In setting forth of such a solemne Toye!
> How would he firke? lyke Adam ouerdooe
> Vp & about? Dyue into Cellars too
> Disguisd? and thence drag forth Enormity?
> Discouer Vice? Commit Absurdity?
> Vnder ye Morall? shewe he had a pate
> Moulded or stroakt vp to suruey a State!
>
> (69–84)[36]

In the 1630s Jonson thinks his creations, Lantern Leatherhead and Adam Overdo, are funny and worthy of laughter; he enjoys his own work. (Moreover, he expects readers of his poem to catch references to his play—more evidence suggesting it had been revived and remained popular.)

Jonson probably held his play back in order to rewrite it. Jonson enjoyed tinkering with his work, as we know; he rewrote *Every Man in His Humour*, added post-production notes to his classical tragedies and masques, and may have revised an early comedy, *A Tale of a Tub*, for production in the 1630s. While the evidence about *Bartholomew Fair* is scant, it suggests that the dramatist left the play out of the 1616 Folio so he could rework it. In 1631, however, he could wait no longer and had to yield to financial necessity.

Ben Jonson suffered a stroke in 1628.[37] This illness left him in financial trouble, and his argument with Jones in 1631 over their masque *Chloridia* led to a loss of income from Court, when Jones used his influence to have Jonson's masques passed over.[38] In 1631

Jonson's financial problems led him to write several letters to the Earl of Newcastle appealing for money;[39] it may also have led him to try publishing some of his as yet unpublished plays.

A folio containing *Bartholomew Fair, The Devil Is an Ass,* and *The Staple of News* was planned and abandoned in 1631.[40] The printer, one John Beale, set up these plays for the playwright's publisher, Robert Allot, and printed the sheets; several copies of the volume were sent to some of Jonson's friends and patrons. Evidently, however, Beale's work was so bad and Jonson's patience so short that the project was given up.

Jonson sent a copy of parts of the work to the Earl of Newcastle with a letter complaining about Beale:

> . . . It is the Lewd Printers fault, that I can send yor Lord, no more of my Booke done. I sent you one peice before, the fayre [i.e. *Bartholomew Fair*], by Mr. Withrington, and now I send you this other morcell, the fine Gentleman that walkes in Towne; the Fiend [i.e., *The Devil Is an Ass*], but before hee will perfect the rest, I feare, hee will come himselfe to be a part, vnder the title of the absolute knaue, wch he hath play'd wth mee; My Printer, and I, shall afford subiect enough for a Tragi-Comoedy. for wth his delayes and vexation, I am almost become blind, and if Heaven be so iust in the Metamorphosis, to turne him into that Creature hee most assimilates, a Dog wth a Bell to lead mee betweene Whitehall and my lodging, I may bid the world good Night.[41]

Beale's work was rich in misspelling, omission, and metathesis and is, unfortunately, the only authoritative text for the play. Although Jonson gave up the task of correcting "the absolute knaue" in 1631, the publisher Robert Allot kept the unissued copies of the plays. Allot died in 1635, Jonson in 1637, and Allot's widow transferred her right to these plays to printers who brought out these editions as a second volume to the *Works* in 1641.[42] Beale's ignorance was triumphant, after all.

# *Bartholomew Fair* Restored: 1660–1700

BARTHOLOMEW *Fair* was popular during the late seventeenth century. Indeed, Noyes says, "None of Jonson's comedies had a more brilliant stage-record during the Restoration than his magnificent *Bartholomew Fair.*"¹ We know of eleven performances in London and one in Dublin; no doubt there were others. (These two cities were the chief markets for drama, since Scotland still forbade acting and there were no established theaters in provincial towns.)² Moreover, the play received critical discussion from such figures as John Dryden, Thomas Shadwell, Edward Phillips, William Congreve, and Thomas Brown.³ Both John Downes and Gerald Langbaine mentioned its success on stage.⁴

Nor is it difficult to account for this success. Jonson's play, even in the Restoration, remained true to the spirit of the medieval fair. Like the Smithfield fair, the play was associated with religious controversy and patronized by royalty. Just as his father and grandfather had, Charles II enjoyed Jonson's plays despite Puritan criticism—as did his court. Initially, at least, the Restoration playhouse audiences were composed of royalists who welcomed Jonson's attack on the Puritans even more than his contemporaries once had. The audience was still royalist—paradoxically, because the country was still Puritan. Less than two years after Oliver Cromwell's death, the citizens of London welcomed back their monarch, but many of the sentiments remained strong that had led to the Commonwealth's closing of the theaters. The advent of sex comedy in the 1670s did nothing to decrease opposition to the stage. These plays were not only more licentious than those of the

Jacobean or Caroline period; they were also often redactions of French or Spanish, that is, Papist, dramas. The plays' subject matter, of course, resulted in even more attacks. Although Jeremy Collier's *Short View of the Immorality and Profaneness of the English Stage* (1698) is the best known of these attacks, it is hardly the first or only one. From the beginning of the Restoration, the city authorities insisted that there be no more than two theaters (despite ingenious attempts by other companies to continue), and even these two patent companies had trouble getting audiences. Puritans attacked the theaters, playwrights seemingly did what they could to prove Puritan charges were true, and only the King's love of playgoing kept the theaters open. When *Bartholomew Fair* was first revived in 1661, the audience which attended plays was pre-selected, as a result, from those who served the King and who hated Puritanism. Such an audience had more reason to dislike Rabbi Busy than the spectators of the Hope Theatre or of James's court. Satire aimed at the hypocrisy of extremist Puritans was certain to please them. By an accident of history, Jonson's satire once again referred to contemporary events.

In addition to *Bartholomew Fair*'s accidental topicality, Jonson was a figure of greater literary importance in the Restoration than in the Renaissance. He served many Restoration playwrights as a model for their own comedies (and occasionally tragedies). Critics greatly admired Jonson's classicism and comedy of humors (elements which twentieth-century critics find less important), and his work became a standard against which the Restoration measured the shortcomings of contemporary dramatists.[5] In particular, Restoration critics often cite his work when they argue about either wit or humor, though, as Robert Hume has pointed out, ". . . this supposedly neat and tidy debate on wit versus humour leads straight to total confusion."[6] The major problem is the inconsistency of terms. A pair of late eighteenth-century critics may agree on Jonson's classicism or his use of humors, but disagree vigorously on his wit. Yet each critic may mean something different by the word "wit."

John Dryden is the most important figure in Restoration Jonson criticism. *An Essay on Dramatick Poesy* remarks on Jonson's use of classical authors with the famous comment, "He was not onely a professed Imitator of *Horace*, but a learned Plagiary of all the others; you track him every where in their Snow."[7] Out of context this criticism sounds hostile; in fact, Dryden valued Jonson's use of classical sources.

As for *Johnson* . . . I think him the most learned and judicious Writer which any Theater ever had. . . . He was deeply conversant in the Ancients, both *Greek* and *Latine* and he borrow'd boldly from them: there is scarce a Poet or Historian among the *Roman* Authours of those times whom he has not translated in *Sejanus* and *Catiline*. But he has done his Robberies so openly, that one may see he fears not to be taxed by any Law. He invades Authours like a Monarch, and what would be theft in other Poets, is onely victory in him. (Berkeley ed., 17:57)

Dryden's praise of Jonson's classicism was echoed almost mechanically by other Restoration critics.[8] But *Bartholomew Fair* is not an overtly classical comedy, save in its observation of the unities. Not surprisingly, it attracted less critical attention than other Jonson comedies, particularly the classical *Epicoene*, which Dryden praised so highly in *An Essay on Dramatick Poesy*.

It was not ignored, however. While primarily concerned with Jonson's more classical (hence, more "correct") plays, Dryden noticed that Jonson imitated the Smithfield fair in the same way that he imitated classical authors:

> In *Bartholomew-Fair*, or the Lowest kind of Comedy, that degree of heightning is used, which is proper to set off that Subject: 'tis true that the Author was not there to go out of Prose, as he does in his higher Arguments of Comedy, *The Fox* and *Alchymist*; yet he does so raise his matter in that Prose, as to render it delightful; which he could never have performed, had he only said or done those very things that are daily spoken or practised in the Fair: for then the Fair it self would be as full of pleasure to an ingenious person as the Play; which we manifestly see it is not. But he hath made an excellent Lazar of it; the Copy is of price, though the Original be vile. You see in *Catiline* and *Sejanus*, where the Argument is great, he sometimes ascends to Verse, which shews he thought it not unnatural in serious Plays: and had his Genius been as proper for Rhyme, as it was for Humour, or had the Age in which he liv'd attain'd to as much knowledge in Verse, as ours, 'tis probable he would have adorn'd those Subjects with that kind of Writing.[9]

This passage shows sensitivity to Jonson's techniques. Dryden notices not only Jonson's conscious decorum in language, but also his use of imitation—whether he was "holding a mirror up to nature" to produce realistic comedy or footnoting the sources when he wrote classical tragedies. Later Restoration critics were less perceptive. In 1699 Thomas Brown wrote about the Smithfield fair:

If antiquity carries any weight with it, the fair has enough to say for itself on that head. Fourscore years ago, and better, it afforded matter enough for one of our best comedians to compose a play upon it. But *Smithfield* is another sort of place now to what it was in the times of honest *Ben*; who, were he to rise out of his grave, wou'd hardly believe it to be the same nuperical spot of ground where justice *Over-do* made so busy a figure, where the crop ear'd parson demolish'd a gingerbread-stall; where *Nightingale*, of harmonious memory, sang ballads, and fat *Ursula* sold pig and bottled-ale.[10]

Brown assumes a greater fidelity to the natural world than Jonson's play offers; Dryden recognizes that the verisimilitude of *Bartholomew Fair* is a by-product of the playwright's imagination. Yet Dryden's position on Jonson was attacked bitterly by other Restoration writers who felt that in one section of *An Essay on Dramatick Poesy* (and later in his essay defending the "Epilogue" of *The Conquest of Granada, II*) Dryden had undervalued Jonson, specifically, that he had failed to acknowledge Jonson's wit.[11]

The most fervent apologist for Jonson was Thomas Shadwell, whom Dryden would later pillory in *MacFlecknoe*. (Shadwell was not alone in criticizing Dryden; he was just more obdurate than anyone else.) Shadwell complained in 1668 that

> . . . I have known some of late so Insolent to say, that *Ben. Johnson* wrote his best Plays without Wit; imagining that all the Wit in Plays consisted in bringing two persons upon the Stage to break Jests, and to bob one another, which they call Repartie, not considering that there is more Wit and Invention requir'd in the finding out good Humour, and Matter proper for it, than in all their smart Reparties.[12]

Shadwell found wit in *Bartholomew Fair:*

> The most Excellent *Johnson* put Wit into the Mouths of the meanest of his People, and, which is infinitely Difficult, made it proper for 'em. And I once heard a Person of the greatest Wit and Judgement of the Age say, That *Bartholomew Fair* (which consists most of low Persons) is one of the wittiest Plays in the World. If there be no Wit required, in the rendering Folly ridiculous or Vice odious, we must accuse *Juvenal*, the best Satyrist and wittiest Man of all the *Latin* Writers, for Want of it. (Preface to *The Humorists, Works,* 1:188–89)

His comments on wit suggest that he would have defined the word much as Dryden once had, that is, that wit "is a propriety of Thoughts and Words; or in other terms, Thought and Words elegantly adapted to the Subject."[13] Like Dryden, Shadwell is here praising Jonson's decorum of language. Perhaps the two were closer in their opinions of Jonson than they realized.

In any case, Dryden continued to insist that Jonson sometimes wanted wit. (One must notice the difference in Dryden's definition of the term in the following remarks.)

> . . . when at any time [Jonson] aim'd at Wit, in the stricter sence, that is, Sharpness of Conceit; [he] was forc'd either to borrow from the Ancients, as, to my knowledge he did very much from *Plautus:* or, when he trusted himself alone, often fell into meanness of expression. Nay, he was not free from the lowest and most groveling kind of Wit, which we call clenches. . . .[14]

Unlike Jonson's Littlewit, Dryden intensely disliked "clenches," that is, puns and quibbles. For Dryden, the chief virtue of *Bartholomew Fair* (or of any of Jonson's works) lay in its excellence of imitation and in its portrayal of humorous characters. On the perfection of Jonson's humor comedy, Shadwell and Dryden could agree. Yet not even on this point was there general assent. Late in the Restoration, William Congreve wrote:

> The character of *Cob* in *Every Man in his Humour,* and most of the under Characters in *Bartholomew-Fair,* discover only a Singularity of Manners, appropriated to the several Educations and Professions of the Persons represented. They are not Humours but Habits contracted by Custom.[15]

Clearly, disagreement about *Bartholomew Fair* is a venerable tradition in Jonson criticism.

Despite the disagreement on what Jonson's virtues were or were not, there was general agreement that Jonson was great. For Restoration critics, Jonson belonged to the Golden Age of the theater; they found their own age merely silver.

One must note that the elements of Jonson's work which appealed to the Restoration were largely *non*dramatic. Generally Jonson's plays (and specifically *Bartholomew Fair*) are *not* praised for their physical comedy, or their satire, or their dramaturgical effectiveness. Jonson's insistence that he wrote works, not plays, had been too effective, perhaps, for his comedies were rarely considered as *dromena,* plays to be performed. John Marston had insisted:

Comedies are writ to be spoken, not read. Remember the life of these things consists in action,[16]

but his good advice was largely ignored by Restoration critics. They regarded *Bartholomew Fair* as a play of secondary importance, ranking behind *Volpone, The Alchemist,* and Dryden's favorite, *Epicoene.* In 1675, Edward Phillips praised ". . . three of his Comedies, namely the *Fox, Alchymist* and *Silent Woman. . . ,*" then added ". . . nor is his *Bartholomew Fair* much short of them."[17] (Today some would argue that this judgment is justified, that Restoration critics were right in regarding *Bartholomew Fair* as inferior to the other three comedies. It is more difficult to account for the high praise Restoration critics often heaped on *Catiline.*)[18]

Whatever critics said, the play was quickly made welcome on the stage. It seems to have been the second of Jonson's plays produced in the Restoration. *Epicoene* had proved successful in 1660, but *Bartholomew Fair* was even more successful throughout 1661.[19] On Saturday, June 8, 1661, Samuel Pepys saw it for the first time and wrote in his diary:

. . . to the Theater and there saw *Bartlemew faire,* the first time it was acted nowadays. It is [a] most admirable play and well acted; but too much profane and abusive.[20]

"The Theatre" was Thomas Killigrew's Theatre Royal at Gibbons Tennis Courts in Vere Street, Clare Market, where the King's Company remained until May of 1663. According to John Downe's list in *Roscius Anglicanus,* "His Majesty's Company of Comedians" (i.e., the King's Company) held the rights to virtually all of Jonson's plays.[21]

Although the cast for this first production of *Bartholomew Fair* (or any of the Restoration performances) is "not known" according to *The London Stage,*[22] Downes does remark that "Mr. *Wintersel,* was good in Tragedy, as well as in Comedy, especially in Cokes in *Bartholomew-Fair;* that the Famous Comedian *Nokes* came in that part far short of him."[23] James Nokes was especially praised for the title role in *Sir Martin Marall* (1667), a play which alludes to *Bartholomew Fair.* According to Nicoll, "Contemporaries say that no one could equal him [Nokes] in the interpretation of a grave English type of folly."[24] Nokes, however, acted for

Davenant's Duke's company, the rivals of Killigrew's King's Company, so he could have taken the role of Cokes only after Wintershall's death in 1679 and the union of the two companies in 1682.[25] Thus, while we have no record of the play's performance between 1674 and 1702, such performances clearly took place—with first Wintershall, then Nokes playing Bartholomew Cokes.

While we know that Wintershall played in these early productions, we can only speculate about the other principal performers in the King's Company and the parts they would probably have played. The two leading actors were Major Michael Mohun and Charles Hart (Shakespeare's grand-nephew). Hart is known to have been particularly handsome; his Jonsonian roles included Catiline and Mosca, two schemers.[26] The role of Quarlous would fit him well. The Cavalier Mohun drew praise for his fine voice, which he used in such roles as Volpone, Face, and Truewit.[27] Insofar as *Bartholomew Fair* has a human protagonist, it is Adam Overdo, and Mohun probably played this role. Another important performer was John Lacy. Lacy seems to have excelled at hyperbolic comedy, to judge by his casting as Falstaff, Sir Politic Would-be, Captain Otter, and Ananias.[28] Given his success in the Puritan role from *The Alchemist*, Lacy surely played Zeal-of-the-Land Busy. When the play was revived in 1661, Walter Clun probably appeared in it. Before his brutal murder after a performance as Subtle in *The Alchemist*, Clun was famous for his performances as Iago, Falstaff, the coward Bessus in *A King and No King*, and the Lieutenant in *The Humorous Lieutenant*.[29] Wintershall, who played Cokes, picked up the role of Subtle after Clun's murder; Clun could well have played Cokes in the original revivals of *Bartholomew Fair*.

Although Killigrew used actresses as well as actors to play women's roles in the 1661 productions, the practice was still very new; little information survives about the actresses. Catherine Corey claimed in 1689 that she had performed for 27 years, so she may have been in some of the early revivals. Corey was noted for her portrayal of Dol Common.[30] Another early actress, perhaps the earliest, was Margaret Hughes, but she is not known to have taken any Jonsonian roles.[31] Finally, Edward Kynaston must be mentioned. Pepys praised Kynaston's performance as Epicoene, and the actor had performed other women's roles as well. After actresses took the stage, Kynaston turned to men's roles such as Peregrine in *Volpone*.[32] Kynaston *could* have played a woman's role in *Bartholomew Fair,* but it is more likely that he played a role like Edgworth, the gentlemanly cutpurse. Corey may have played Grace.

To conclude, Pepys may have seen the following performers in the early revivals of *Bartholomew Fair:* Adam Overdo—Michael Mohun; Zeal-of-the-Land—John Lacy; Quarlous—Charles Hart; Cokes—Walter Clun, followed by William Wintershall and James Nokes; Edgworth—Edward Kynaston; Grace—Catherine Corey.

Despite Pepys's strictures on the play's profanity and abuse, the production he saw did not include the puppet show with its humiliation of Rabbi Busy. (He saw the puppetless version again on June 27.)[33] The puppets were first introduced when Pepys saw the play on September 7, 1661. He was not amused.

> So I having appointed the young ladies at the Wardrobe [i.e., Lord Sandwich's daughters] to go with them to a play today, . . my wife and I . . . took them to the Theatre, where we seated ourselfs close by the King and Duke of Yorke and Madam Palmer (which was great content; and endeed, I can never enough admire her beauty); and here was *Barthlemew fayre,* with the Puppet Shewe, acted today, which had not been these forty years, (it being so satyricall against puritanisme, they durst not till now; which is strange they should already dare to do it, and the King to countenance it), But I do never a whit like it the better for the puppets, but rather the worse.
>
> Thence home with the ladies, it being, by reason of our staying for the King's coming and the length of the play, near 9 a-clock before it was done. (2:173–74)

(Performances generally began around 3:30 in the early Restoration, but in this case the actors held the curtain until Charles II arrived.)[34] Pepys saw the play with the puppet show again on November 12, but it still annoyed him:

> with Sir W. Pen, my wife and I, to *Barthlemew fayre,* with puppets (which I had seen once before, and the play without puppets often); but though I love the play as much as ever I did, yet I do not like the puppets at all, but think it to be a lessening to it. (2:212)

Pepys had expressed surprise that the King did "countenance" the attack on Puritanism which so shocked him, but evidently the Restoration audience not only countenanced, but welcomed it. Theatregoers considered Puritans fair game, and few seemed to share Pepys's reservations.

Five performances of *Bartholomew Fair* are recorded in 1661. Of these, four were the productions Pepys saw at the Theatre Royal and the fifth was a performance by the King's Company on December 18, 1661, which Sir Henry Herbert lists. In addition to these five performances, King Charles evidently saw a comedy entitled *The Play of the Puritan,* which may have been *Bartholomew Fair* but was, more likely, based closely on Jonson's play.

On October 12, the Puritan William Hooke wrote a friend, giving an indignant description of *The Play of the Puritan.*

You will heere by the bearer of the play of the Puritan before the Highest [Charles], where were present (as they say) the E: Manchester & 3 Bpps, and London one of them. In it were represented 2 Presbiterians vnder the forme of Mr. Baxter & Mr. Callamy, whose Habitt & actions were sett forth: prayers were made in imitation of the Puritan, with such scripture expressions as I am loath to mention, the matter such as might have beene vsed by any godly man in a right maner: The case of Syon lying in the dust was spreade before, &c: & God's former deliverances of his peo: vrged in such phraises as would amaze yow if yow heard them, with eyes lifted vp to heaven, one representing the Puritan put in the stockes for stealing a pigg, & the stockes found by him vnlockt, which he admires at as a wonderfull p[ro]vidence & fruite of prayer, vpon which he consults about his call, whether he should come forth or not, & at last p[er]ceived it was his way, & forth he comes, lifting vp his eyes to heaven, & falls to prayse & thankesgiving; I canot tell yow all of it, being large, but such as that some prsent, who were farr from liking the Puritan, were grtly astonished, wondring the house did not fall vpon there heades. The play I heere, was taken out of one or two of Ben. Johnson's &c: for which Ben. would say, that, if he were damn'd, it would be for these 2 playes. I heere it hath beene acted againe. Playes are grtly frequented by the greatest, but Lectures are like to goe downe.[35]

Hooke believed *The Play of the Puritan* was "taken out of one or two of Ben. Johnson's," obviously *Bartholomew Fair,* possibly conflated with *The Alchemist.* Hooke's description of the action does not match what happens to Busy in *Bartholomew Fair,* but it comes close, and Hooke was writing a hearsay account. While Busy steals no pig in Jonson's play and wastes little time in leaving the stocks behind, he is put in the stocks and regards his escape as a miracle. The letter suggests that there were two Puritans (as in *The Alchemist*) and that the performers imitated Richard Baxter and

Edmund Calamy, two distinguished Presbyterian divines. (This imitation of celebrity was not unique in the Restoration: Catherine Corey, when she played the treacherous Sempronia in *Catiline*, gave a scandalous imitation of Lady Harvey, which led to her arrest. Lady Castlemain, an enemy of Lady Harvey, secured Corey's freedom for another performance—given under a rain of oranges.)[36] The satire on the Puritans elicited Hooke's surprise as well as his indignation. If Hooke's information is correct, Charles and some of his court were particularly sympathetic to those anti-Puritanical portions of *Bartholomew Fair*. Puritan sympathizers, however, found the play deeply offensive; while the court audience admired the accuracy of Jonson's satire, Puritans like Hooke were outraged at the way Rabbi Busy represented Puritan behavior. In part, the mixed reaction to the play is a question of verisimilitude. One group thinks Jonson is accurate, the other thinks him inaccurate. But Hooke (or Pepys) is less upset by Jonson's hostile portrait than by the audacity of presentation and the relish with which royal circles received the play. During its first Restoration revivals, the play provided one of London's strongest reminders about the radical shift of power. Those who were generally neutral were "greatly astonished" at the King's sanction of the play, particularly the puppet show, which so startled Pepys with its daring.

There was a marked decline in productions of *Bartholomew Fair* after 1661, but its first year of revival had been an exceptional success. Fear of a revival of the Puritan Commonwealth quickly dissipated, however, and with it went some of the need that Restoration audiences at the Theatre Royal had initially felt to mock Puritan hypocrisy. As the play lost its topicality, it also lost some audience interest, particularly since Restoration taste in comedy preferred the problems of young lovers. Grace Wellborn lacks warmth and is easily wooed by Winwife. Moreover, she is a minor character in comparison to Celia or even Epicoene. Quite aside from changing tastes in religion and romance, however, there were practical considerations which limited the play's success.

In 1662 Sir Edward Browne saw the play at "the New Theatre in Lincolnes Inne fields," that is, at Killigrew's Theatre Royal in Vere Street.[37] Although Browne does not give the date of this production or record his reaction to it, he does note that his admission cost one shilling, sixpence. This cost is a marked increase over that of the Renaissance production at the Hope. Jonson's Induction tells us that the cheapest admission at the Hope was sixpence; as Waith points out, "the scale of prices given [in the Induction] is much higher than usual, possibly because *Bartholomew Fair* was a new play in a new house" (190). Usually in the Renaissance, spectators were admitted to the pit for a penny and to the Gentlemen's Room for as much as sixpence. In the Restoration, the cheapest admissions were to the upper gallery for a shilling and to the middle gallery (where Browne probably sat) for one shilling, sixpence. Admission to the pit (the term is used differently from the way it was in the Renaissance) cost half a crown or two shillings, sixpence, while a box (the equivalent of the Gentlemen's Room) was four shillings.[38] The rise in prices is noticeable. No wonder Pepys often commented guiltily on his extravagance in attending the theater. These high prices were, in part, the reason for the smallness of Restoration audiences. Even though only two patent theaters operated, there were not enough spectators to fill both houses. The competition between Killigrew and Davenant for the audience was intense and relied largely on novelty.

Not only did *Bartholomew Fair* fail to satisfy the managers' need for novelty and the changing tastes of Restoration audiences in comedy, but it also failed to meet Restoration tastes in staging. One of the play's strengths is the simplicity of a unified locale; a company needs only booths to set up the fair. But Restoration audiences did not want simplicity of setting, no matter how much lip service critics paid to the classical unities. Instead they wanted variety and spectacle. The next recorded reference to a production of *Bartholomew Fair* makes this clear. Pepys went to Killigrew's new theater in Bridges Street on Tuesday, August 2, 1664:

> . . . to the King's play-house and there saw *Bartholomew fayre*, which doth still please me and is, as it is acted, the best comedy in the world I believe. I chanced to sit by Tom Killigrew—who tells me that he is setting up a Nursery; that is, is going to build a house in Moore fields, wherein he will have common plays acted. But four operas it shall have in the year, to act six weeks at a time—where we shall have the best Scenes and Machines, the best Musique, and everything as Magnificent as is in Christendome; and to that end hath sent for voices and painters and other persons from Italy. (5:230)

Clearly Pepys enjoys Jonson's play; clearly he is *more* interested in the proposed theater which will offer "everything as Magnificent as is in Christendome." Killigrew's plan came to nothing, but the source of his ambition is easy to name: William Davenant.

Initially Killigrew's company enjoyed greater success than Davenant's. Killigrew began with the performance rights to many popular Renaissance plays, while at first Davenant had the rights to only a few old plays.[39] Killigrew's company had such experienced actors as Mohun, Hart, and Lacy; Davenant used novices. Killigrew could perform Renaissance plays as they were; when Davenant was finally granted nine of Shakespeare's plays, it was with the condition that he make changes in them.[40] But Davenant turned his weaknesses into strengths. He had greater control over his company because he had more experience than they did. He changed such Shakespeare plays as *The Tempest* by making them more congruous with late seventeenth-century taste for music and elaborate staging. Finally, Davenant capitalized on his experience by introducing changeable scenery. In 1663, when Killigrew's Theatre Royal moved from Vere Street to Bridges Street, the new building had provisions for scenery; already Killigrew was trying to catch up with Davenant.

Killigrew continued to offer pre-Restoration plays, such as *Bartholomew Fair*, which had proved popular, but the bulk of his efforts was directed to new, fashionable productions which would compete with Davenant's company for spectators' money. *Bartholomew Fair* required no scenery or special effects and used simple ballads lacking operatic grandness. In addition, its topicality quickly faded. It no longer reflected the London scene, and yet it was of too recent a vintage to be regarded as an interesting anachronism. There were only four more recorded performances in London before 1700 and one in Dublin. Yet these scattered performances are among the most interesting in the play's history.

The first of these performances is mentioned in the Lord Chamberlain's list as one of the plays "His Ma[te] . . . hath had presented before him."[41] The entry indicates that the company received 10 pounds when the play was performed on April 27, 1667 at the Theatre Royal in Bridges Street. (The Theatre Royal in Bridges Street burned in 1672 and the Drury Lane Theatre was erected on its site.) Charles had seen the play before, of course, on September 7, 1661, and he had watched *The Play of the Puritan* as well before October 12, 1661. Obviously the King retained a taste for Jonson's comedy and his preference is responsible for three of the four London performances between 1665 and 1700. In addition to the 1667 performance, Charles also watched the play on February 22, 1669 at court and on November 30, 1674 (the location for this performance is uncertain, but probably was the Drury Lane Theatre).[42] As Noyes has remarked, "the number of performances commanded by Charles II supports the popular tradition that the comedy was one of his favorite plays."[43] Perhaps Charles continued to find the satire on Puritans fresh.

Pepys too continued to go to the play, although he had reservations about its performances. When he saw the 1669 performance at the Cockpit in Whitehall, he wrote:

> . . . in the evening I do carry them to White-hall, and there did without much trouble get into the playhouse there, in a good place among the Ladies of Honour, and myself also sat in the pit; and there by and by come the King and Queen, and they begun—*Bartholomew fayre.*—but I like no play here so well as at the common playhouse. Besides that, my eyes being very ill since last Sunday and this day sennit with the light of the candles, I was in mighty pain to defend myself now from the light of the candles. (9:456)

Playhouse conditions at court were clearly inferior to those at the Drury Lane Theatre, at least as far as Pepys with his poor sight was concerned. Aside from lighting, the Cockpit was probably ill-suited for Italianate scenery in comparison to the Drury Lane Theatre. From Pepys's remarks it would therefore seem that *Bartholomew Fair* was normally performed with scenery of some sort, though it would not, of course, be so elaborate as that of contemporary productions designed specifically for extravagant scenery.

Pepys was uncomfortable not only with the performance conditions, however; the satire on the Puritans continued to annoy him. After going to the Smithfield fair on September 4, 1668, he took his wife to the Theatre Royal in Bridges Street:

> . . . my wife having a mind to see the play, *Bartholomew fayre* with puppets; which we did, and it is an excellent play; the more I see it, the more I love the wit of it; only, the business of abusing the puritans begins to grow stale, and of no use, they being the people that at last will be found the wisest. (9:299)

Once again Pepys condemns the puppet show. He does so for two reasons: first, it "grows stale" and is unfashionable; second the Puritans "will be found the wisest" and therefore the satire is inaccurate. The problem of fashion was, of course, one reason that the play was less and less produced in the late seventeenth century. But the issue of accuracy is an important one: once again, the question of verisimilitude arises.

So far as Restoration critics were concerned, Jonson's greatest strength as a playwright lay in his ability to mirror London society in his comedies and to re-create Roman society in his tragedies. It was his skill as a portrait painter which drew their admiration. But this play and *The Alchemist*, unlike his others, remained disturbingly topical in their satire on Puritans and raised questions about the truth of Jonson's realism. The chief problem was simply whether Jonson's portrait of the Puritans was accurate in showing them as greedy hypocrites. The importance of this question tended to obscure the Restoration's perception of the play, because, by focusing on Jonson's accuracy, the critics overlooked any other issues in *Bartholomew Fair*. Ironically, one of these ignored issues was Jonson's emphasis on *how* a spectator ought to understand his play. In the Induction, Jonson had tried to defend himself against the charges that his satire was based on real people and that his play was profane. Again and again the play warns the audience that appearance is deceptive, and it concludes by announcing that those who would judge others should "remember you are but Adam, flesh and blood! You have your frailty." But this good advice was forgotten by those, like Pepys, who found Jonson's satire embarrassing as well as those, like Charles, who may have enjoyed it maliciously.

Some Puritans, who disliked the play because it did not reflect a reality which they acknowledged, expected bad art to be punished—if not by man, then by God. For example, in *The Theatre of God's Judgements* (1597), the influential Puritan author, Dr. Thomas Beard, had listed instances from history of God's direct intervention in the world to reward or punish men.[44] (Beard was well-known, but his pupil, Oliver Cromwell, is more famous.) Hooke, in his letter about *The Play of the Puritan* (1661), had said that the less enthusiastic members of the court audience were left "wondering the house did not fall upon their heads." In 1670, a Dublin theatre did exactly that, and commentators were quick to point out the divine justice of the disaster.

In a letter from Dublin dated December 27, 1670, Robert Bowyer sent Robert Southwell word of the disaster.

> Yesterday there being very many people at the playhouse the lofts fell down, three or four killed dead in the house, whereof a maid of Mr. Savage's was one. My Lord Lieutenant was hurt a little, one of his son's much hurt, the Countess of Clanbrasill ill hurt, very many wounded, some of which it is said cannot live. The play that was acted was Bartholomew Fair, in which it seems there is a passage that reflects

upon a profession of holiness, and it is said when they were entering upon that part the scaffold fell.[45]

Bowyer thinks the play is probably profane, but Southwell remained unconvinced. Fifteen years later Southwell wrote his son, praising the play's reflection of reality in order to make a moral point:

> Dear Neddy,
>
>     I think it not now so proper to quote you verses out of Persius, or to talk of Caesar and Euclide, as to consider the great theatre of Bartholomew Fair, where, I doubt not, but you often resort, and 'twere not amiss if you cou'd convert that tumult into a profitable book. You wou'd certainly see the garboil there to more advantage if Mr. Webster and you wou'd read, or cou'd see acted, the play of Ben Jonson, call'd Bartholomew Fair. . . . I fancy then you will say—*Totus mundus agit histrionem.* . . ."[46]

Southwell, unlike Bowyer, sees the play as a moral document, not a profane one. For him the play's relationship to the real world is not controlled by divine intervention but by human observation. But Bowyer was not alone in reporting this *post hoc, ergo propter hoc* thinking. So did the Puritan, Richard Baxter, who used the playhouse collapse as an example of a divine rebuke to sinful man.

Nine years earlier, Hooke reported that in the 1661 production of *The Play of the Puritan* one of the characters was gotten up "under the form of Mr. Baxter." Evidently the 1670 Dublin production had repeated this joke. In *Reliquiae Baxterianae*, Baxter himself gives more detail than Bowyer.

> There happened a great rebuke to the Nobility and Gentry of *Dublin* in *Ireland*, which is related in their *Gazette* in these words. [*Dubl. Dec.* 27. "Yesterday happened here a very unfortunate Accident: Most of the Nobility and Gentry being at a Play, at a publick Playhouse, the upper Galleries on a sudden fell all down, beating down the second, which together with all the People that were in them, fell into the Pit and lower Boxes: His Excellency, the Lord Lieutenant, with his Lady, happened to be there, but thanks be to God escaped the Danger without any harm, part of the Box where they were remaining firm, and so resisting the Fall from above; only his two Sons were found quite buried under the Timber. The younger had received but little hurt, but the eldest was taken up dead to all appearance, but having presently been let Blood, &c. recovered. There were many dangerously hurt, and seven or eight killed outright.]

So far the *Gazette*. About seventeen or eighteen died then, and of their Wounds. The first Letters that came to *London* of it, filled the City with the report, that it was a Play in scorn of Godliness, and that I was the Person acted by the Scorner, as a Puritan, and that he that represented me was set in the Stocks, when the fall was, and his Leg broke. But the Play was *Ben Johnson's Bartholomew-Fair*, with a sense added for the times, in the which the Puritan is called a *Banbury* Man, and I cannot learn that I was named, nor medled with more than others of my Condition, unless by the Actor's dress they made any such reflecting Intimations.[47]

Baxter certainly had no trouble understanding the connection between the actual world and the way it was represented on stage. The stage was a part of the actual world and as such was controlled by God. God was offended by the play and administered "a great rebuke." Profanity in the playhouse, like profanity in the street, might be punished by Him at any moment.

Quite aside from Puritan aesthetics, the question of verisimilitude in Jonson's work assumed more importance in the late seventeenth century. Just as the orthodox critics all praised his classicism, so they all praised the way in which he imitated the actual world. Yet, perversely, Jonson's acknowledged verisimilitude cost him popularity, particularly when a critic coupled Jonson's imitation of the actual with a comparison to Shakespeare's plays. As Noyes points out, "If the critics were fond of emphasizing Jonson's imitation and his inferiority to Shakspere, they were equally fond of remarking that his plays were out-of-date and that revivals merely discouraged writers of new plays."[48] In the case of *Bartholomew Fair*, audiences after the 1660s felt less and less amused by Jonson's fairground, more and more uncomfortable with his Puritans. In addition, after 1685 Jonson's plays drew little royal patronage. James II was struggling to keep his crown and had little time for the theater. Protestant successors never showed the same enthusiasm for Jonson that James I or Charles II had. For thirty years the play was performed infrequently. There was a flurry of revivals from 1702 to 1722; the imitation of life which the critics prized was not so topical, and hence not so troublesome. But critical tastes were changing as well, and *Bartholomew Fair* would soon die.

If Jonson's play suffered for its verisimilitude in the late seventeenth century, it was not altogether ignored. Thomas D'Urfey used the play because of its verisimilitude in his poem, "Collin's Walk through London and Westminster" (1690).[49] Poor Collin is a country cousin seeing the sights of London. When he is taken to the theater, he watches "An Ancient Comick Piece they knew, / Intitled the Fair of *Bartholomew*," (148). Collin is at first puzzled by the play, then mistakes Jonson's fiction for reality and assumes he is at a Puritan meeting led by Zeal-of-the-Land Busy. At first he admires Busy, then he is annoyed by the audience's jeers, and finally when Busy is put in the stocks:

> In *Breast* a suddaine Anger glow'd,
> And instantly revenge he vow'd,
> As thinking this a base affront,
> To the whole Tribe of those that Cant. . . .
>
> (150)

Collin assails the stage, lecturing the audience in Busy's defense. The play comes to a halt because:

> The Actors when he first begun
> By th' Noyse were stopt from going on;
> Nor was the Audience less amaz'd,
> Who all on *Collins* out-side gaz'd;
> Who now possess't with zealous Rage,
> Was getting up upon the Stage,
> With Sword in Hand resolv'd on War,
> With those who stock'd the Presbiter. . . .
>
> (151–52)

A "Blew Coat Bully" stops Collin's assault by thumping him on the head, to the audience's delight. Collin recovers and tries to prove his worth by showing the audience he has a purse filled with gold. This display just makes the audience laugh harder, Collin grows more heated, and the situation seems sure to become more violent. All is saved, however, when

> . . . a Female Wastcoateer,
> Came up, and whispering in his Ear,
> The ill-match'd Combatant draw[s] off,
> Leaving the Crowd to showt and laugh.
>
> (153)

D'Urfey's poem, like Jonson's play, is fiction and one would be ill-advised to mistake either for actual events. The point is not how well Jonson's play was acted in 1690, how brilliant the performances must have been to make Collin confuse the playhouse with a

Presbyter meeting. Instead one should note that D'Urfey thinks Jonson's *Bartholomew Fair* in performance would offer enough realism for it to be plausible that Collin, as stupid as Cokes, could mistake an actor for a Puritan. The joke does not revolve around an actual performance; it does depend on the play's reputation for verisimilitude. A playwright could have worse tributes.

# The Play at Drury Lane: 1700–1735

THEATRICAL records are sketchy for the last quarter of the seventeenth century, so we have no idea how often *Bartholomew Fair* was performed. Certainly it was neglected at the turn of the century, but by 1702 it was once again part of the repertoire.[1] All we can safely say is that *Bartholomew Fair* enjoyed fifteen years of performance at the beginning of the Restoration, that it was probably neglected for twenty-five years until 1702, and that it was popular for the first quarter of the eighteenth century. This record seems odd, but it offers an accurate reflection of what was happening in the London theater. The features of the play that had contributed to its strength in the Renaissance and Restoration once again assumed importance. In the first quarter of the eighteenth century, *Bartholomew Fair* not only suited the changing needs of a London company, but also regained its topicality. Finally, the literary critics of the period took a renewed interest in Jonson, regarding *Bartholomew Fair* as a minor, but acceptable, work.

Let me begin with the changes in the theater. During these years the play's stage history is closely linked to the history of the Drury Lane actors. Always an actors' play, *Bartholomew Fair* prospered as the performers began to control the theaters; therefore, to understand what happened to the play, one must also understand the rapidly changing world of the theater.

In the forty years between 1660 and 1700, a revolution had taken place in the theaters. Some of the changes are well-known: the introduction of women on stage, the loss of the thrust platform stage, the shift to spectacular effects. Another revolution took place in playhouse audiences and their tastes.[2] In the first few years of the Restoration, the audiences were largely aristocratic and cheerfully immoral. Charles II enjoyed the theater and it enjoyed his protection. This privileged audience, however, was too small to support two royal theaters. By 1682, the King's and Duke's Companies joined together, and this United Company continued, with sex comedies by playwrights such as Aphra Behn, as well as heroic dramas by Otway and others. This union cut the demand for playscripts in half; although Renaissance plays were still revived, the United Company had less need of them as Restoration dramatists built a contemporary popular repertoire. When the company did produce Renaissance dramas, management often tailored these plays to suit the new audience's tastes. In a discussion of Shakespearian adaptations during these years, George Odell points out that

> The second group [of adaptations], several years later (1678–82), concerned itself with plots of historical subject, whether classical or English, and pressed into service certain plays of romantic or mythical interest that lent themselves with greater or less readiness to connection with the troublous political times in those very years of Charles II's reign.[3]

Clearly, at about the time the two companies united, they chose to appeal to their audiences by combining the traditional drawing power of the Renaissance dramatists with the newer tastes for heroes, romance, and topicality. Beaumont and Fletcher were widely produced, Shakespeare underwent revision, and Jonson suffered neglect. Considering the scarcity of heroes and romance in Jonson's plays, this neglect is unsurprising. The records are not good, but in the years from 1677 to 1700, we know of only one definite Jonson production: *The Silent Woman (Epicoene)*, performed by the United Company in 1685.[4] In 1691 Langbaine did say that *Bartholomew Fair, Catiline, The Alchemist,* and *Every Man in His Humor,* as well as *Epicoene,* were still acted; however, he may have been referring to earlier productions, done in the 1660s and early 1670s.[5]

The playhouse revolution did not stop when the companies united; it moved on and, as the theaters continued to change, the fortunes of *Bartholomew Fair* were to rise again. Charles II had protected the theaters, but James II had more pressing concerns. In 1688, when William and Mary came to power, social reform came

to the theaters, so that theatrical offerings in the decades that followed became more decorous, a process which led eventually to
the sentimental comedy of the eighteenth century.[6] The United
Company came under Christopher Rich's control. A parsimoni-
ous man, Rich ignored the agreements which the actors had with
management, and his dealings dissatisfied the performers. Led by
the great actor, Thomas Betterton, the actors bolted in 1695 and set
up a rival company to Drury Lane. This second playhouse rein-
troduced the old problem of repertoire: each of the two theaters
had to draw wider audiences or both would fail. Increasingly, the
companies appealed to respectable middle-class tastes instead of
limiting themselves to court circles. The actors' revolt was comple-
mented by a second event, the publication of Jeremy Collier's *A
Short View of the Immorality and Profaneness of the English Stage*
(1698). Again, the companies were forced by public opinion to
conform with more sedate, middle-class tastes. The revival of
*Bartholomew Fair* in 1702 probably occurred because of the actors'
revolt and because of Collier's attack (which I discuss later in this
chapter).

With two companies, the number of contemporary plays available to each was effectively divided in half. The companies tried to
fill out this dearth by bringing in foreign entertainers and divertis-
sements, and also by staging a spate of revivals, particularly of
Renaissance comedies. According to Odell:

> Gildon's Comparison between the Two Stages [sic] (1702) humorously
> recounts the contest between Betterton and Rich at their rival houses,
> with Betterton praying for aid to Shakespeare, and Rich to Jonson,
> whose comedies he drew up as "Battalia against *Harry* the 4th and
> *Harry* the 8th" at the other theatre.[7]

During 1700, Betterton's company produced, in addition to the
*Harry*s, an opera based on *Measure for Measure;* while the Drury
Lane company revived *Volpone* and *Epicoene* and put on Cibber's
version of *Richard III.* Lansdowne adapted *The Merchant of
Venice* in 1701 for Betterton; and the following year John Dennis
performed a similar service, using *The Merry Wives of Windsor,* for
Rich at Drury Lane. Moreover, in 1701–2 Drury Lane continued
to perform *Volpone* and *Epicoene* and added *The Alchemist* (also
revived by Betterton) and *Bartholomew Fair.*[8]

Although no cast list survives for the Drury Lane production on
June 3, 1702, the advertisement promised that "all the Parts [are]

Acted to the best Advantage."[9] Those actors who had performed in the play in the Restoration had retired, and Betterton had taken most of the better actors with him when he left in 1695. Still, Drury Lane was not without good actors after the division.[10] George Powell stayed with Christopher Rich, taking over many of Betterton's roles; John Mills, Colley Cibber, and John Verbruggen were all beginning their careers at Drury Lane. The actor Joseph Williams and the comedienne Mrs. Mountford (later Verbruggen) quickly left Betterton and returned to Rich, while Robert Wilks also returned, from Dublin. Ben Johnson (not related) and William Bullock soon joined the Drury Lane company as novices. These actors were all at Drury Lane seven years after the division, when *Bartholomew Fair* was first revived. A number of these actors are named in later cast lists of *Bartholomew Fair:* Powell, (Quarlous, 1708); Mills (also Quarlous, 1707); Cibber (Busy, 1707); possibly Wilks (Winwife, 1718)[11]; Johnson (Wasp, 1707); and Bullock (Cokes, 1707).[12] These facts suggest that the Drury Lane advertisement was no lie and that the parts were indeed acted "to the best advantage." A revival of this production in the following month (August 18, 1702) supports the conclusion that the revival was successful.

Other productions at Drury Lane followed: two in the 1703–4 season and two in the 1704–5 season. Although the cast lists for these performances have not survived, the company's reputation for skillful comedy may account in part for the play's continuing in the repertoire.[13] Certainly the play must have made some profit, or the tight-fisted Rich would have dropped it; on the other hand, it did not meet with overwhelming success, or another company than Drury Lane would have performed it. It was, in short, quite typical of the moderately successful play, even to the advertisements that bolstered the offering of a play "Written by the Famous Ben Johnson." with the added treat of "Dancing and Singing" after the play. Offering more entertainment than a mere play could provide was a recognized means of winning a bigger audience.

However, despite his constant desire to increase his proceeds, Rich overlooked an obvious piece of timing. None of the productions between 1703–5 coincided with the actual fair, so none profited from public interest in Smithfield. Oddly enough, both of the 1702 productions *were* played in the summer, and the one scheduled for August 18 even coincided with the fair. That August performance was a benefit for Mrs. Lucas, who may have had a hand in choosing the play or setting its dates, since actors' benefits were normally in the spring.[14] Perhaps actors were more aware than Rich was of the upcoming fair at which many of them performed; more likely he saw no reason to provide his performers with free publicity before they began their off-season work in the fairground booths. This attitude seems short-sighted, but Rich's dealings with his actors were often characterized by myopia.

In fact, the story of Rich's downfall revolves around his quarrels with performers. Rich lost control of the Drury Lane company in a complicated series of financial maneuvers which took place between 1706 and 1707. First Rich pretended to give up power to Owen Swiney; then he was forced out of Drury Lane by the actors who took over the management for themselves. *Bartholomew Fair*'s production history reflects these two upheavals in management, for during this period the play was faithfully linked to the actors of Drury Lane—even when they were not in Drury Lane. Thus in 1707 the play received four performances in an unsuitable theater: the Haymarket.

The Haymarket was a relatively new theater at the time, having been built by John Vanbrugh for Betterton's company. (In 1705 Betterton transferred his license to Vanbrugh and remained with the company solely as an actor.)[15] Problems soon arose, particularly with regard to the acoustics. As Cibber wrote:

> This [theater's] extraordinary and superfluous Space occasion'd such an Undulation from the Voice of every Actor, that generally what they said sounded like the Gabbling of so many People in the lofty Isles in a Cathedral—The Tone of a Trumpet, or the Swell of an Eunuch's holding Note, 'tis true, might be sweeten'd by it, but the articulate Sounds of a speaking Voice were drown'd by the hollow Reverberations of one Word upon another.[16]

To compound the difficulties, the theater stood at that period in a pasture, which was well outside of town and difficult for its audience to reach.[17] Finally, the actors who had revolted with Betterton were growing old; many had retired, and those who remained were no longer at their peak. Given these circumstances, Vanbrugh wanted a reunion with Rich's Drury Lane company.[18]

Cannily, Rich realized the strength of his position with an established company and a good playhouse. Therefore, he refused a union, forcing Vanbrugh to lease the Haymarket Theatre, company, license, and scenery to Owen Swiney for five pounds each acting day. Swiney was a friend of Rich's and the two of them seem to have made a secret agreement. While Rich tried his hand with the more fashionable—and profitable—opera at Drury Lane, Swiney took his choice of the Drury Lane actors to the Haymarket by October, 1706. He also took *Bartholomew Fair.*

In August of the 1706–7 season, Swiney's actors performed the play three times. (It was performed again at the Haymarket in the following October.) The timing of the August performances was undoubtedly intended to capitalize on the opening of the Smithfield fair. Evidently the timing worked, so the production enjoyed success—despite the theater's disadvantages—to judge from the number of performances and the play's speedy revival in the autumn. By producing the play in August, Swiney made it topical.

The fair with which Jonson had grown up had changed by 1707, though Jonson would probably still have felt at home there. For the purposes of this study, the most important change was the expansion of the entertainment offered at the fair. As religious conflict diminished at the fair when the Puritans lost power, the kinds of entertainment increased. Not only were there puppets and rope-dancers of the sort that Jonson might have seen; actors practiced their trade in the fairgrounds once again, just as they had done in the Middle Ages. As Morley points out:

> From among the actors at Drury Lane, there was always at this time a strong body detached for performance at the Fair, where there was more money to be earned than in the theatre. For this reason, and not because they began the world as strolling showmen, it has to be said of not a few good actors, that they performed in booths at Smithfield.[19]

Many actors tried to stretch their income by moving between playhouse and booth. Of those who performed in *Bartholomew Fair* in 1707 and after, at least eight also performed at the fairground booths.[20] Scheduling performances in August served two purposes: it drew in spectators who were interested in the fair and it meant that actors performing at the fair received some free publicity.

Cast lists survive from the 1707 summer performances. These early eighteenth-century lists name several actors in *Bartholomew Fair* who also performed at Bartholomew Fair: John Mills, William Bullock, Benjamin Johnson, and Henry Norris.[21] (Another actor, George Pack, performed in both play and fair, but he seems not to have gone to Smithfield until 1717.)[22] In Jonson's play, Mills took the role of Quarlous, Bullock of Cokes, Johnson of Wasp, and

The Play at Drury Lane: 1700–1735 85

Norris of Littlewit. Other actors in the 1707 run are named also: Overdo—Theophilus Keen; Winwife—Benjamin Husband; Edgworth—Barton Booth; Busy—George Pack; Ursula—Mr. Cross; Nightingale—Henry Fairbank; Grace—Mary Porter; Purecraft—Mrs. Powell. Although the play had not been performed for two and a half years, some of the actors had undoubtedly been in those early eighteenth-century performances and so were not new to the play. The identity of these more experienced actors is germane.[23] They were Mills, Bullock, Johnson, and Norris—the same performers who had a vested interest in the play's success since they were also the ones who performed at the fairground. Nor can one overlook the fact that these four played leading roles. *Bartholomew Fair* may well have been revived at their suggestion and urging because it could enhance their profits at the booths. The real question here is whether the inexperienced Swiney would have allowed the actors such a prominent role in managing the company. Yet the situation was not without precedent; as Emmett Avery has pointed out:

> In the summer the management frequently turned the house over to the young actors, who played two or three times weekly until the Fairs began.[24]

In short, the actors probably revived the play for their profit, and possibly for their pleasure as well. It is, after all, an actor's play—exceptionally suited to ensemble performance, sympathetic to actors' concerns, and filled with good character speeches. Unlike plays written as vehicles for one strong performer, *Bartholomew Fair* allows most of the actors in a company to shine, without exhausting the ability or strength of any one actor.

However, this strength of the play is a weakness for the stage historian. Although the play was a popular one during this period, its ensemble form means that no single actor stood out and became identified with a role as Cibber did with Lord Foppington or Charles Macklin with Shylock. Thus no anecdotes about eighteenth-century performers in the play remain to delight later readers. Moreover, the roles were often, though not always, performed by a *series* of actors. For example, the romantic lead, Winwife, was played in turn by Husband, Bickerstaff, Elrington, Quin, and Wilks; while the comically eccentric Rabbi Busy was taken first by Pack, then Cibber, then Bickerstaff, and continued to revolve among these actors until 1722.

The changes may have grown out of the chameleon fortunes of the Drury Lane Theatre between 1707 and 1710.[25] During the 1707–8 season, Colonel Henry Brett quietly acquired a share of the management of Drury Lane, and in December, 1707, he acted to take half of Rich's power. Moreover, the Lord Chamberlain insisted that the actors had to return to Drury Lane and that the Haymarket was to be reserved for musical performances, including opera. By April Brett had handed over his authority, though not his profits, to the triumvirate: his old friend and drinking companion, Colley Cibber; the Irish tragedian, Robert Wilks; and a comedian, Richard Estacourt, whose place was soon taken by Thomas Doggett. That summer, under the mixed management of Rich and the triumvirate of actors, there were three productions of *Bartholomew Fair*. Clearly, when the actors began to take a part in the company's management, as they certainly did in the 1707–8 season and probably did in 1706–7, they presented the play more frequently than Rich had when managing by himself. Further, they presented it during the summer when it would have more topical appeal for the audience and thus advance the actors' interests.

In addition, the cast lists suggest that the actors recognized that one of the play's strengths was an ensemble piece. One can see that the new hybrid management juggled with the casting, although one of the cast lists has not survived. For example, Husband had played Winwife in all the 1707 productions. The role was given to Bickerstaff in the July, 1708 production; but by August Husband was playing it again. The casting of Busy was also changed. Pack played it three times in 1707, but the last performance in 1707 had Cibber in the role. Perhaps Cibber was unsuccessful or his new management responsibilities took too much time, but in the first summer performance of 1708, Pack played the role again. Bickerstaff, who had played Winwife, played Busy in the last performance of 1708. There are other, similar, shifts in casting; a major shakeup seems to have occurred for the final 1708 performances when there were six casting changes. The fluidity of these changes underlines the fact that the play has no star characters; actors could learn new parts easily and be shifted from role to role as it suited the needs of the company. The play has no true human protagonist. This is an artistic fact about the work, but it is a practical fact as well in the world of the playhouse.

The role juggling probably does not signal disagreement among the management. Rich may have been fighting with the actors, although he seems to have been more busy in maneuvering to regain his power than in running the company. Cibber's comment on the season suggests that any changes were made agreeably to strengthen the company, not out of rancor or dissatisfaction. In his *Apology*, he writes:

> It may easily be conceiv'd, that by this entire Reunion of the two Companies Plays must generally have been perform'd to a more than usual Advantage and Exactness: For now every chief Actor, according to his particular Capacity, piqued himself upon rectifying those Errors which during their divided State were almost unavoidable. Such a Choice of Actors added a Richness to every good Play as it was then serv'd up to the publick Entertainment: The common People crowded to them with a more joyous Expectation, and those of the higher Taste return'd to them as to old Acquaintances, with new Desires after a long Absence. In a word, all Parties seem'd better pleas'd but he who one might imagine had most Reason to be so, [Rich] the (lately) sole menaging Patentee. (2:56)

The actors thrived when the companies were reunited, and *Bartholomew Fair*, an actors' play, thrived with them. However, Rich's displeasure soon drove the actors and the play out of the Drury Lane Theatre once more, though his actions led to his eventual downfall.

At this stage, Rich's actions move from the complicated to the Byzantine.[26] To summarize quickly, he used a legal scheme to draw profits away from Drury Lane, involved Brett in a lawsuit brought by Sir Thomas Skipwith, and by the spring of 1709 had driven Brett out of management—thereby vitiating the power that Brett had given the triumvirate of actors. Rich celebrated this victory by bullying the actors, who sought redress by appealing to the Lord Chamberlain and who also planned with Owen Swiney to move the company to the Haymarket. The actors succeeded in both plans. In June, 1709, the Lord Chamberlain sent Rich a Silence Order; "all the confederated Actors immediately walk'd out of the House, to which they never return'd 'till they became themselves the Tenants and Masters of it."[27] This return was in 1710 and with it the actor-manager tradition returned to British theater.

Once the actors took over their own management, *Bartholomew Fair* was performed regularly, though not so often as before. As a glance at Noyes's Appendix will show,[28] the actual number of Jonson plays performed did not increase radically, but the way in which Jonson was scheduled did change. Under Rich, the company might offer two Jonson productions in a season (1701–2;

1705–6) or it might offer nine (1703–4). In the troubled seasons from 1706 to 1711 when the management shifted from hand to hand and the actors moved back and forth between Drury Lane and the Haymarket, the number of Jonson productions increased, perhaps because they were familiar and could be relied on to bring in a respectable number of theatergoers. Thus, although Rich scheduled only two productions in 1705–6, once the actors moved to the Haymarket under Swiney in 1706–7, the number of productions jumped to eight. The following season, during the shift back to Drury Lane, there were nine productions, and in 1708–9 there were twelve. When the actors went back to the Haymarket in 1709–10, there were seven productions and the next season there were seven more. In the following years the number of Jonson productions fell off, but *Bartholomew Fair* was performed at least once a season until the 1723–24 season.

During these years the play's casting continued to vary a little, though never as radically as it had done in 1708. As older actors retired or left the company, their roles were handed to younger actors. For example, when a new theater was opened in December, 1714 at Lincoln's Inn Fields, a number of *Bartholomew Fair*'s mainstays deserted Drury Lane: Theophilus Keen (Overdo); William Bullock (Cokes); George Pack (Busy, alternating with Cibber); and Francis Leigh (perhaps Joan Trash).[29] Their places were taken by Mr. Miller as Overdo, Mr. Shepard as Cokes, and John Bickerstaff who alternated the role of Busy with Cibber during the play's 1715 production. This production was also James Quin's first known appearance in the play; he took the role of Winwife. For the most part, however, the picture we get from the records is of a reliable play, placidly produced, which gradually fell out of fashion.

Looking at the records, one sees an increase in the number of peripheral entertainments offered with Jonson's play to draw in audiences. The bills for *Bartholomew Fair* advertise "Morrice Dances" (1712), a "Mimic Song of the Country Life" (1715), singing and dancing (1717), *Harlequin Turn'd Judge* (1718), *The Dumb Farce* (1719), and *The Escape of Harlequin* (1722).[30] But the audiences seem to have been fond of Jonson's fair. The advertisements often claim ingenuously that the play is presented "at the particular Desire of several Ladies of Quality" and in one case *Bartholomew Fair* replaces another play, *The Unlucky Lover; or the Merry London Cuckolds*, which had been advertised (July 16, 1717).[31] Twice Jonson's comedy was performed for George, Prince of Wales (later

George II), "By His Royal Highness's Command" (December 10, 1716 and December 21, 1722).[32] Since most of the performances took place during the summer, though, the play's lasting strength for the Drury Lane company was its familiarity and its topicality, i.e., its connection with the yearly Smithfield fair.

After 1722 the play was performed only twice. Nine years later, on George II's birthday, October 30, 1731, Cibber, Wilks, and Booth revived it for one performance.[33] Only Mr. Shepard as Overdo and Ben Johnson as Wasp had performed in it before; the others were new. Two of the new actors were the sons of men who had acted in the play many times: Theophilus Cibber played the role of Cokes and William Mills succeeded his father John Mills as Quarlous. Another piece of casting worth note is Miss Raftor who played Win Littlewit; this actress became better known as Kitty Clive. Evidently the play's success (or failure) was not notable since any comment about it has disappeared; however, the play was not revived in that summer nor for the next few seasons.

In August 1735, it was, unfortunately, revived at Lincoln's Inn Fields. Again, no comment on the production survives, but the cast list speaks volumes; it mentions such characters as Ananias, Valentine, Rover, Silence, Florella, Loveit, and Pickle Herring. Advertisements mention the singing and dancing performed with it and invite the audience to watch Mrs. Charke and Miss Brett dance the *Black Joke*.[34]

After this performance of *Bartholomew Fair*, itself a kind of *Black Joke*, the play went unperformed for almost two hundred years. Its eighteenth-century popularity was short-lived. That popularity grew out of the play's suitability for the needs of the Drury Lane actors, but it would be absurd to think that the actors' concerns were the only reason it held the stage for twenty-five years. No matter how much the actors liked the play, it would certainly have failed unless it appealed to the audience's taste. That taste was increasingly genteel, and *Bartholomew Fair*, like another successful revival, *The Alchemist*, was not over-burdened with gentility. Their success, then, seems paradoxical. A resolution of the paradox comes out of the eighteenth century's changed attitudes toward Jonson's work and the theater as a whole. Although Jonson was recognized as a major literary figure in the Restoration, few discussions of his work had focused on its morality, save those of the Puritans, who found his satire offensive and called it wicked. When the debauchery of Restoration comedy drew critical attention, however, critics also directed their attention to Jonson and his contemporaries and found the old Renaissance plays more moral than their own.

Jeremy Collier, a High Churchman and a Nonjuror, is easily the best known of those who attacked Restoration comedy. His *Short View of the Immorality and Profaneness of the English Stage* (1698) had enormous influence both in itself and in the controversy it engendered. Though not a Puritan, he attacked theater with all of a Dissenter's zeal. The stage was impious, profane, and obscene; clergymen were abused by their portrayal on the stage and this treatment of the clergy was both unprecedented and unreasonable. For some reason, though, Collier and those who followed him felt partial toward Jonson, despite his excesses. Collier's arguments deserve close examination.

In his first chapter, Collier dismisses Shakespeare to get to Jonson:

> As for *Shakespear,* he is too guilty [of lewdness] to make an Evidence: But I think he gains not much by his Misbehaviour; He has commonly *Plautus's Fate,* where there is most Smut, there is least Sense.
>
> *Ben Johnson* is much more reserved in his *Plays,* and declares plainly for Modesty in his *Discoveries.* . . .[35]

Collier then quotes extensively from *Discoveries* and announces that he might quote more, "but that may serve for an other Occasion."

This other occasion occurs in the fourth chapter which says that

> . . . *Ben Johnson* in his Dedicatory Epistle of his *Fox* has somewhat considerable upon this Argument [about artistic purpose]; And declaims with a great deal of zeal, spirit and good Sense, against the Licentiousness of the *Stage.* (P. 157)

Two pages of quotation from Jonson follow to confute one of Collier's targets, John Dryden: "Why then if *Ben Johnson* knew any thing of the Matter, Divertisement and Laughing is not as Mr. *Dryden* affirms, the *Chief End* of *Comedy*" (p. 159). Dryden is also attacked for his play *The Mock Astrologer,* a play, Collier claims, that glorifies wickedness. Dryden had argued that in this play he was simply following the practices of earlier playwrights, specifically Ben Jonson in *The Alchemist.* Collier seems infuriated by this claim and spends several pages (151–54) explaining that there is nothing immoral in *The Alchemist, Epicoene,* or *Volpone.*

While no modern critics doubt that Jonson *is* a moral play-wright, neither would they accept Collier's definition of morality. By his standards, Jonson's work ought to be at least questionable. Yet Collier always defends Jonson. For example, Collier's response to what he conceives to be Dryden's attack on Jonson seems a case of special pleading. Face, says Collier, never actually counsels Lovewit to debauch Dame Pliant; Lovewit's marriage may possibly be honorable; in the epilogue Lovewit and Face apologize for their actions. Clearly Collier wants his readers to regard Face and Lovewit as reformed and virtuous characters, but this conclusion strains credulity if one has bothered to read *The Alchemist*. (Even more puzzling is Collier's early remark [p. 78] that a wicked Restoration character is modelled upon Jonson's Tribulation Wholesome. Surely this is inconsistent with his later argument for the morality of *The Alchemist*.) Collier's defense of *Epicoene* grows yet more peculiar. He altogether ignores Dauphine's plot against Morose and the scenes in which the mock clerics debate divorce, though these would seem to be clear support for his argument against the stage. (Again, in earlier remarks Collier discusses these episodes and rationalizes their presence. He is consistent in his inconsistency.) Instead Collier points out that although Dauphine claims to be in love with the Collegiate Ladies, he never consummates a relationship. Collier concludes ingenuously, "*Dauphin* therefore is not altogether so naughty as this Author [Dryden] represents him" (p. 153).

When he can, Collier leaps to defend Jonson as an exemplar of morality, even if this means ignoring troublesome scenes or twisting motives to rationalize misconduct. *Bartholomew Fair* is scarcely mentioned. In part this may be because the play was less popular than the others, but it *was* performed and it *does* contain some of the "profane" elements that draw his fury when they occur in Restoration comedy. Nor did he simply overlook immorality in Renaissance authors: he did rebuke Shakespeare; he also suggests either that Francis Beaumont reformed in character or that John Fletcher wrote all the sordid sections of their work ("Their Hand," he comments, "was not always steady.") But *Bartholomew Fair* is mentioned only once, in connection with Vanbrugh's *The Relapse*, and that comment is curiously indulgent.

Collier abominates John Vanbrugh's plays. In a discussion of Vanbrugh's *The Relapse* (p. 109), Collier pronounces the play's conclusion "insolently Profane." He goes on to remark ironically that, "The spirit of this thought [i.e., Vanbrugh's] is borrow'd form [*sic*] *Ben Johnson's Bartholomew Fair;* only the Profaneness is mightily improved, and the Abuse thrown off the *Meeting-House,* upon the *Church.*" In other words, Vanbrugh "improves" Jonson by intensifying the profanity; moreover while Jonson only attacked the Puritans and the Meeting-House, Vanbrugh goes much further in mocking the Established Church of England. Later in this same section, Collier surveys the ways that Shakespeare, Jonson, and Beaumont and Fletcher treat the clergy. Shakespeare and Beaumont and Fletcher come in for some criticism, though nothing so severe as Vanbrugh receives. Jonson goes virtually uncensured. The abuse of clergymen in *Epicoene* is deemed excusable; the "untoward" priests in the late plays are forgivable since Jonson created them in his dotage; the Puritans in *The Alchemist* and *Bartholomew Fair* are unmentioned.

At the beginning of the eighteenth century, Jonson was considered the most respectable of English playwrights—at least in Collier's opinion. Since Collier was the most severe critic of the English stage, to say this is to say a great deal. The question of why Collier approved of Jonson remains unanswered and perhaps unanswerable when one considers Collier's untempered and warm enthusiasm in arguing Jonson's case. Certainly Collier shows great admiration for classical authors, and in this he reflects the neoclassical age in which he wrote. Jonson had a reputation as the most classical of the Renaissance dramatists, which undoubtedly worked to his advantage. (It would be interesting to know what Collier thought of Chapman.) Another strong point in Jonson's favor was his attack on Puritans. Though Collier, like the Dissenters, excoriated the stage, he was a good High-Churchman who disliked and distrusted Puritans. So far as Collier was concerned, Jonson was impeccably orthodox. Finally, Jonson was not only a moral playwright, but a vocally moral playwright: he flaunted his morality in his prefaces, in *Discoveries,* and in the prologues. Jonson's beliefs in didacticism and drama's moral function may unsettle some modern critics, but Collier delighted in them.

The approval lavished on Jonson's comedies by Collier and those who followed him may have made Jonson a useful author for the Drury Lane company in the early years of the eighteenth century as they struggled to free themselves from Rich and to establish their power. *Bartholomew Fair* not only answered critics who found the playhouse immoral; it was actually approved by those same critics. Further, Jonson's plays are actable, designed to show performers to their best advantage, as recent critics have begun to notice. In this connection, one might note that although *Bartholomew Fair* lost its place in the repertoire, other Jonson plays—*Epicoene, Volpone, The Alchemist, Every Man in His Humor*—continued to prosper for many seasons. Yet even these plays went unperformed in the late eighteenth and nineteenth century. *Bartholomew Fair,* in some ways the most characteristic of Jonson's plays, was simply the first to die.

## [ 6 ]

# "Out-o'-the-way, Far-fetched, Perverted Things"

LONDON'S fair had begotten Jonson's play, but Smithfield out-lived its offspring. After 1735 the play went unperformed, while the fair continued shakily until 1855. By the 1750s the city authorities were moving to clean up the fair; plays were forbidden by 1762.[1] Although the fair held on for almost another century, the London Corporation imposed more and more restrictions on it and its death in the nineteenth century was long overdue. Tastes were changing in the eighteenth century, and both the play and the fair met with increasing hostility: they were too rowdy and no longer suited their customers.

*Bartholomew Fair* was the first to fail. The play had prospered on stage because of its actors; it also fell out of favor because of the actors, or rather because of one actor, David Garrick. The actor-manager system, which had begun with the triumvirate at Drury Lane, soon became the star system with the advent of Garrick. His powerful position at Drury Lane meant that his taste controlled that theater's repertoire. Garrick had a taste for Jonson, so London saw his versions of Jonson's plays: *The Alchemist, Epicoene, Every Man in His Humor;* these plays, which he popularized, were *the* Jonson plays produced.[2] Only the ever-popular *Volpone* could continue on stage without Garrick's assistance.[3]

Garrick considered reviving *Bartholomew Fair,* but did not. While he was staying at his country house in Hampton, he was visited by Dr. John Brown. Brown was a clergyman, best remembered today for *An Estimate of the Manners and Principles of the*

94

*Times* (1757); in the *Estimate,* he had included a compliment to Garrick as "a great genius" who had restored to the stage "the fulness of its ancient Splendor."[4] (Certainly he had reason to think well of Garrick's taste since Drury Lane had produced Brown's plays, *Barbarossa* in 1754 and *Athelstane* in 1756.)[5] While Brown and Garrick were talking in the garden at Hampton, Garrick suggested that Brown revise *Bartholomew Fair* for production. Brown began to do so in the summer of 1765. On August 10 he wrote of the play:

> [Its] comic merit, in point of *character,* is universally allowed to be of the first degree. In point of *plan,* it goes on well upon the whole, till the third or fourth act, and then falls into nonsense and absurdity. This, I really think, I have removed; retaining, at the same time, every the least scrap of what is thinly scattered through the bad parts of it, such as might be worth preserving. This is all I pretend to: and as to the excellence of the other parts, it is generally allowed to be supreme. The Pig-woman certainly cannot be removed without spoiling the whole; for on *her* depend all the fine comic scenes between Busy, John Littlewit, and Justice Overdo; as well as some of Coke's and Wasp. [*sic*] In short, she is the *great connecting circumstance* that *binds* the *whole together.* If the scene of her scolding be thought rather too coarse, it may easily be softened. . . . You will oblige me much if you can bring on either of these pieces this season.[6]

Brown's choice of Ursula as "the *great connecting circumstance*" is an interesting one, for in the early eighteenth-century productions, the character seems not to have been considered central. The actor playing the role often goes unidentified in the cast lists, while the role was omitted altogether in the 1735 burlesque production at Lincoln's Inn Fields. Evidently Garrick had also wanted to omit the Pig-woman, on account of coarseness, while Brown disagreed. Yet a later letter shows that Brown was not remaining altogether faithful to Jonson's play.

> I pique myself more on rectifying this plan, than on any plan I ever struck out in my life. It is amazing to think how any writer could do so well, and so ill, at the same time, as Ben Jonson did in this comedy. However, so far as I am a judge, there are admirable materials left, enough to make out a first-rate comedy after the trash is thrown out. But I will not anticipate. As to the little connecting scenes which I have added, I have made them as short as possible, because I know that my comic composition is nothing. As soon as you have well considered it, let me have your thoughts. I can furnish you with some songs that will

be proper for the purpose: that which is inserted is the finest that ever
Purcel composed; and if Miss Wright can *act it* as well as she can *sing it*
(for both will be necessary), that very song will draw an audience. You
will see that I have struck out four of the *dramatis personae*. . . .[7]

We shall never know who the four characters were that Brown cut,
for Garrick was probably the only one to see Brown's work. The
adaptation has disappeared, as have Garrick's replies to Brown.
Certainly it was never produced, though one can understand why
Garrick made his original suggestion. As Noyes points out, "Perhaps the play seemed as likely to succeed as *Every Man in His
Humor*, or perhaps the suppression of the fair made a revival of the
comedy seem desirable."[8]

Garrick's motives for not going on with the revival are less clear.
Brown's adaptation of the play, evidently into a musical, may have
been poor. Garrick's health may also have been a factor. That fall
he wrote to Richard Berenger:

You know I had some time ago labour'd so much, that I was oblig'd to
retire from the fatigues of the Theatre, (By the order of Doctor Barry
& others) to recruit my Self abroad; I was unluckily seiz'd with a
Malignant Fever in Germany that fell upon my Spirits, and tho' I am
now much better than I was, yet I fear the double business of Manager,
& Actor, would be too violent for me, & therefore I had determin'd
from Necessity to give up Acting; as the pursuing both might have
disagreeable Consequences—[9]

Such a consideration might well have dissuaded him from attempt-
ing a major revival. Perhaps Brown would have placed his version
of *Bartholomew Fair* elsewhere had he lived. On account of a
bizarre train of events, he did not. At about this time, Brown
became involved in a correspondence about Russian civilization, a
subject on which he knew very little. What he said, however,
caught the attention of Catherine the Great, who invited him to
visit her in Russia. Eager to go, Brown was bitterly disappointed
when his poor health prevented the journey. Brown was never a
very stable man, and the next month he cut his throat.[10]

If Garrick did not produce *Bartholomew Fair*, none of his contemporaries were likely to do so. Quite simply, he knew Renaissance drama far better than anyone else working in the theater of
his day. As one scholar reminds us, "His knowledge of those plays
so far surpassed that of his contemporaries that writing has been
assigned to him because it contained borrowings from old plays

that Garrick would know; and the borrowings in his known writings prove how well he knew English and French drama."[11]

It is, of course, simplistic to lay *Bartholomew Fair*'s failure only at David Garrick's feet. There were other factors as well. The eighteenth century's taste in comedy changed quickly and radically. In his essay, "Corbyn Morris: Falstaff, Humor, and Comic Theory in the Eighteenth Century," Stuart Tave points out:

> The metamorphosis of Falstaff was one expression of the general development of comic theory, practice, and criticism in the eighteenth century. The movement was, broadly speaking, from a theory that assumed human nature to be naturally evil to one that assumed it to be naturally good. . . . In practice, this movement produced sentimental comedy, but also Sir Roger de Coverly, Parson Adams, my uncle Toby, and the Vicar of Wakefield. In criticism it preferred Horace to Juvenal, Menander to Aristophanes, Terence to Plautus, Farquhar to Congreve, Addison to Swift, and most important, Shakespeare to Jonson.[12]

The change in the public's idea of what constituted comedy brought disaster for Jonson and his plays. When "the new comic ideal, humanitarian and benevolent, was innocent good humor, good nature, and cheerfulness" (Tave, 102), *Bartholomew Fair* stood little chance of success. No doubt Garrick, had he revived it, would have emphasized Cokes and his party rather than the darker fairground characters, just as he built up Abel Drugger to the detriment of Doll, Subtle, Face, or Mammon.[13] (Perhaps this is why he wanted to eliminate Ursula.) Cokes, after all, does represent innocence and good humor, albeit with an empty head. Yet even if Garrick had produced the play, there is every likelihood that such a revival would have enjoyed as little success as his ill-fated *Epicoene*.[14]

One has little difficulty finding support for what Tave says in the critical attacks that Jonson drew in the eighteenth century. As Shakespeare was being idealized, Jonson was anathematized. A startling amount of vitriol was expended. Because Jonson's plays were unlike Shakespeare's, they were considered badly done, and (or so some eighteenth-century critics reasoned) bad art sprang out of bad character. When proof of bad character was sparse, the solution to the problem was simple: invent the proof. Thus in 1748, Garrick's rival Charles Macklin announced the "discovery" of a nonexistent pamphlet, "Old *Ben's Light Heart* made Heavy by Young *John* [Ford]'s *Melancholy Lover*."[15] The immediate cause of Macklin's forgery was personal gain, since the hoax was "compounded out of tears and flapdoodle by Macklin in order to puff his own forthcoming revival of a play by Ford."[16] But behind this motive is the period's genuine antipathy to Jonson, upon which Macklin drew. The pamphlet purports to be a Caroline attack on Jonson's character in response to his persecution of Ford, Shakespeare's successor. Describing the pamphlet, Macklin charged:

> *Ben* was by nature *splenetic* and *sour;* with a share of envy (for every anxious genius has some) more than was warrantable in society. . . .
> This raised him many enemies, who towards the close of his life endeavoured to dethrone *this tyrant,* as the pamphlet stiles him, out of the dominion of the theatre. And what greatly contributed to their design, was the *slights* and *malignances* which the *rigid Ben* too frequently threw out against the *lowly Shakespeare,* whose fame since his death, as appears by the pamphlet, was grown too great for *Ben's envy* either to *bear* with or *wound.*
> It would greatly exceed the limits of your paper to set down all the *contempts* and *invectives* which were uttered and written by *Ben,* and are collected and produced in *this pamphlet,* as unanswerable and shaming evidences to prove his *ill-nature* and *ingratitude* to *Shakespeare,* who first introduced him to the *theatre and fame.*[17]

Macklin's forgery was exposed, rather reluctantly, by Edmond Malone, but it was not unique. In 1753, five years after Macklin's pamphlet, Robert Shiells doctored the *Conversations with Drummond.* Evidently Drummond's brusque and unflattering description of Jonson's character was too mild for Shiell's taste, so he simply inserted a sentence he felt Drummond *ought* to have said, making it appear that Drummond had, in fact, said it:

> [Jonson] was in his personal character the very reverse of Shakespear, as surly, ill-natured, proud and disagreeable, as Shakespear with ten times his merit was gentle, good-natured, easy, and amiable.[18]

Again the forgery was exposed; again the exposure did no good. Jonson was burdened with an envious and surly disposition, in which the critics and editors of Shakespeare delighted. If Jonson were envious, he attacked Shakespeare. If he attacked Shakespeare, the eighteenth century could defend the Bard. Defending one's favorite author offers far more amusement than acknowledging the merits of an unsympathetic dramatist who is out of tune with the taste of the period; therefore, Jonson needs must attack Shakespeare.

Shakespeare's editors attacked Jonson in return, and *Bartholomew Fair* achieved prominence as a prime example of Jonson's vicious nature and unpleasant art:

> In the Induction of Bartholomew Fair, . . . three of [Shakespeare's] plays, and in the piece itself two others are attempted to be *ridiculed.*[19]

The number of Shakespeare's plays attacked in Jonson's comedy becomes a point of ambiguity; according to the critics' mood, the Induction ridicules *The Tempest, The Winter's Tale, Titus Andronicus,* and all of Shakespeare's history plays, while the body of the play mocks *Julius Caesar, King Lear,* and *Twelfth Night.*[20] Moreover, the play was an attempt to ridicule Inigo Jones as well, or so it was said, and Walpole comments on the quarrel with Jones: "Whoever was the aggressor, the turbulent temper of Jonson took care to be most in the wrong."[21] Jonson's nineteenth-century editor, William Gifford remarks that *Bartholomew Fair* was "a popular piece, but chiefly remarkable for the obloquy to which it has given birth."[22] There is truth in this. Again and again the eighteenth-century scholars ignored the play's merits to comment on its malice. By the end of the century, Jonson's reputation was at its lowest point.

The change in taste was faithfully reflected on stage where virtually none of Jonson's plays survived. The fact that any of Jonson's plays were staged as long into the nineteenth century as they were was a tribute to the skill of the older actors' performances; as these actors retired and died, their successors refused to perform such old-fashioned, and ill-natured, plays.[23]

At no point in the stage history of *Bartholomew Fair* to this date had the literary quality of the drama played any part in its popularity on stage—or in its rejection. Critics, hostile or not, saw *Bartholomew Fair* as a simple entertainment; indeed, they regarded most of Jonson's work this way. The idea that Jonson's comedies were profound artworks seems almost to have died with Dryden, and even he had found little to praise in *Bartholomew Fair.* Jonson's lost "Apologie" suggests that he considered the play important, but no one at this period concurred. In fact, the literary quality of his plays, so different from that of Shakespeare's more "Romantic" drama, was disdained on those rare occasions when quality rather than the cult of personality was considered. One might think that the early years of the nineteenth century and the triumph of Romanticism would drown Jonson completely. In fact, his rehabilitation began, and with it a growing respect for his work that has led twentieth-century critics and audiences to a new understanding of *Bartholomew Fair.*

The first to speak up effectively for Jonson was Charles Lamb. In his anthology, *Specimens of the English Dramatic Poets Who Lived about the Time of Shakespeare* (1808), Lamb began to revive interest in Shakespeare's contemporaries. To be sure, Bardolatry is part of Lamb's motive; he hopes to show "how much of Shakespeare shines in the great men his contemporaries, and how far in his divine mind and manners he surpassed them and all mankind."[24] Nonetheless, Shakespeare's "enemy" Jonson receives more space than any other dramatist except John Fletcher. Lamb's taste ran to the lyrical and dramatic, at the expense of comic and satiric qualities, and nothing from *Bartholomew Fair* is included. However, Lamb is the first to ignore or contradict the general accusations against Jonson. He denies Jonson's pedantry and praises his "poetical fancy and elegance of mind"; Jonson's character is questioned only once, when Lamb argues that Mammon and his "arrogant pretension" are a Jonsonian self-portrait.[25] After the harshness of Malone, Steevens, Davies, and others, Lamb's mildness and obvious admiration of Jonson come as a shock.[26]

A greater shock followed. Octavius Gilchrist and William Gifford, appalled at the treatment of Jonson, took on his defense. In the same year that Lamb brought out his anthology, Octavius Gilchrist published *An Examination of the Charges Maintained by Messrs. Malone, Chalmers, and Others, of Ben Jonson's Enmity, &c. towards Shakespeare* (1808). The title describes the work well. Gilchrist examines each of the charges made against Jonson's character and explodes all of them; Jonson was officially declared innocent. Gilchrist's work was followed by William Gifford's edition of Jonson in 1816. Gifford wanted more than a verdict of innocence; he wanted vengeance on the prosecutors who had dared to act as judges as well—in particular, he wanted Malone's blood. The edition is magnificently slashing, with most of the skirmishing done in the footnotes. Gifford's response to the charges that Jonson maligned Shakespeare is contempt for the accusers and frequent reference to Gilchrist. He catches Malone contradicting himself, fudging dates, and putting together "a medley of absurdity and falsehood."[27] Typical is Gifford's reaction to Malone's accusation (probably quite warranted), "Ben Jonson had ridiculed the Winter's Tale [in *Bartholomew Fair*] in 1614." Gifford responds:

Mr. Malone had first fixed the date of this play [Winter's Tale] in 1594, then in 1604, afterwards in 1613, and, as far as I can understand him, (for his text and his notes confound each other,) ends with placing it in 1601 or 1602. Still, however, the main ground for all these dates respectively is its having been *sneered* at by Ben Jonson.[28]

Gifford defends Jonson's character, his relationships with other dramatists, even his appearance. Yet he is less eager to defend the quality of Jonson's art.

Gifford regards *Bartholomew Fair* as a humor play and a successful one. In his discussion of the play, Gifford makes an important point:

Many humours and modes of common life are neither amusing in themselves, nor capable of being made so by any extraneous ingenuity whatever: the vapourers in *Bartholomew Fair*, and the jeerers in the *Staple of News* are instances in point.—But further, Jonson would have defeated his own purpose, if he had attempted to elicit entertainment from them: he wished to exhibit them in an odious and disgusting light, and thus to extirpate what he considered as pests, from the commerce of real life. It was in the character of the poet to bring forward such nuisances as interrupted the peace, or disturbed the happiness of private society; and he is therefore careful to warn the audience, in his occasional addresses, that it is less his aim to *make their cheeks red* with laughter than to feast their understanding, and minister to their rational improvement. . . .

There is yet another obstacle to the poet's popularity, besides the unamiable and uninteresting nature of some of his characters, namely a want of just discrimination. He seems to have been deficient in that true tact or feeling of propriety which Shakespeare possessed in full excellence. He appears to have had an equal value for all his characters, and he labours upon the most unimportant, and even disagreeable of them with the same fond and paternal assiduity which accompanies his happiest efforts.[29]

This discussion is at once characteristically nineteenth-century and strikingly original. Gifford perceives that Jonson's comedy is serious, and he is the first student of Jonson since Dryden to make this point. Yet his comments on Jonson's faults show Gifford falling into the very trap he had labored so hard to dismantle: Jonson is criticized for not writing like Shakespeare. When applied to *Bartholomew Fair*, Gifford's comments show his lack of understanding about the play's structure. In that play, all characters are "disagreeable" and necessary to achieve Jonson's serious intent.

Because the fair is the protagonist and the "unimportant" characters are necessary to flesh out the fair's ambiance, Jonson did indeed labor upon them assiduously. Gifford's squeamishness about Jonson's *dramatis personae* characterizes critical attitudes during the nineteenth century. Although Gifford seems not to have known Schlegel's *Course of Lectures on Dramatic Art and Literature*, Schlegel had anticipated much of what Gifford said.

The *Course of Lectures* was published in Germany in 1808, the same year that Lamb championed Jonson's poetry and Gilchrist defended his reputation. But, of course, Schlegel knew nothing of these works, so he not only repeats the canards on Jonson's character, but also complains:

> His pieces are in general deficient in soul, in that nameless something which never ceases to attract and enchant us, even because it is indefinable. . . . He is everywhere deficient in those excellencies which, unsought, flow from the poet's pen, and which no artist, who purposely hunts for them, can ever hope to find.[30]

Perhaps had Schlegel known of Gilchrist's and Lamb's books, he would have revised his opinions, but given the innate lack of sympathy which a Romantic sensibility feels for Jonson's classicism and satire, one must doubt it. Schlegel's other criticisms about Jonson parallel Gifford's comments: Jonson wrote comedy of character (a dangerous belief when one reads *Bartholomew Fair*), and, although his observations were painstaking and accurate, they were too labored.

> Even where he had contrived a happy plot, he took so much room for the delineation of the characters, that we often lose sight of the intrigue altogether, and the action lags with heavy pace. Occasionally he reminds us of those over-accurate portrait painters, who, to insure a likeness, think they must copy every mark of the small-pox, every carbuncle or freckle.[31]

This is Gifford's charge about "a want of just discrimination" in different language. With this approach to Jonson, a critic must dislike *Bartholomew Fair*, and Schlegel does, calling it "nothing but a coarse *Bambocciate*," a picture of low life.[32] He praises Busy, but finds the play unconnected and vulgar.

These attitudes persisted throughout the nineteenth century. After the contentiousness of Gifford, criticism of Jonson, and specifically of *Bartholomew Fair*, features a numbing consistency.

Again and again one reads that Jonson is a great playwright but that the critic finds him unsympathetic. As Hazlitt disarmingly remarks, "There are people who cannot taste olives—and I cannot much relish Ben Jonson, though I have taken some pains to do it, and went to the task with every sort of good will."[33]

Nor is this antipathy surprising. Jonson was generally perceived as a grinding pedant who was not Shakespeare. Leigh Hunt complains of his classicism:

> A classical education may have given him an accidental inclination towards [classical authors], as it will do with most poets at first; but it seems likely that nothing but a perversion of the love of originality, and perhaps a consciousness that he could never meet Shakespeare in equal terms in the wall of humanity, determined him on being a local humorist in the grave cloak of a scholar. What he wanted, besides the generalizing power, was sentiment.[34]

According to Hunt, Jonson's work can only be understood with respect to Shakespeare's, since Jonson wrote in response *to* Shakespeare. To modern ears, most of what Hunt says sounds odd, but his opinion was not at all unusual in his own day. From a different perspective, Schlegel makes the same charge:

> The production of [Jonson's plays] was attended with labour, and unfortunately it is also a labour to read them. They resemble solid and regular edifices, before which, however, the clumsy scaffolding still remains, to interrupt and prevent us from viewing the architecture with ease, and receiving from it a harmonious impression.[35]

The taste of critics had clearly changed, since it was Jonson's classicism and thoroughness that had brought him praise during the Restoration from critics like Dryden.

*Bartholomew Fair* can hardly be said to suffer from a surplus of classicism, though negative critics continue to belabor the point that Jonson is too thorough in his treatment of corruption. Another Romantic criticism—which still haunts critics of the play—is the insistence that Jonson's characters are poorly developed. Hazlitt was particularly hard on Jonson's characters:

> Shakespeare's characters are men; Ben Jonson's are more like machines, governed by mere routine, or by the convenience of the poet, whose property they are. [Shakespeare's] humor (so to speak) bubbles, sparkles, and finds its way in all directions, like a natural spring. In

Ben Jonson, it is, as it were, confined in a leaden cistern, where it stagnates and corrupts; or directed only through certain artificial pipes and conduits, to answer a given purpose.[36]

As usual, Jonson must pay highly for not being Shakespeare. It comes as no surprise that Hazlitt dismissed so unShakespearian a play as *Bartholomew Fair.*

Bartholomew Fair is chiefly remarkable for the exhibition of odd humours and tumbler's tricks, and is on that account amusing to read once.[37]

The wonder is that he read it at all!

Coleridge was kinder than Hazlitt, but his complaint about Jonson's work is essentially the same:

The observation I have prefixed to the *Volpone* [the play is "painful" because none of the major characters is good] is the key to the faint interest which these noble efforts of intellectual power excite, with exception of the fragment of the *Sad Shepherd;* because in that piece only is there any character with whom you can morally sympathize.[38]

Yet Coleridge, unlike many other Romantic critics, took the trouble to separate Shakespeare and Jonson. He points out that Jonson wrote "with a diverse object and contrary principle" to Shakespeare, and, although he prefers Shakespeare, he remarks, "The more I study [Jonson's] writings, I the more admire them."[39] A perception such as this suggests that Jonson's fortunes were on the upturn, as indeed they were.

Though Jonson's work was regarded with increasing favor during the nineteenth century, *Bartholomew Fair* continued to make critics uneasy. It was a sordid play. Several critics remark on Jonson's verisimilitude, his realism, but seldom with unmixed approval. The Romantic sensibility wants a realism which re-creates rather than represents the world. They felt Jonson had not re-created the world because they disliked the world he showed them. Jonson's preference for a grubby, middle-class London failed to enchant or even amuse—and *Bartholomew Fair* is aggressively grubby. As Hazlitt says, "In Ben Jonson, we find ourselves generally in low company, and we see no hope of getting out of it."[40]

An analogue to the usual Romantic attitude toward *Bartholomew Fair* may be found in Wordsworth's reaction to the Smithfield fair:

. . . that ancient festival, the Fair
Holden where martyrs suffered in past time,
And named of St. Bartholomew; there, see
A work completed to our hands, that lays,
If any spectacle on earth can do,
The whole creative powers of man asleep!—
· · · · · · · · · · · · · · · ·
All moveables of wonder, from all parts,
Are here—Albinos, painted Indians, Dwarfs,
The Horse of Knowledge, and the learned Pig,
The Stone-eater, the man that swallows fire,
Giants, Ventriloquists, the Invisible Girl,
The Bust that speaks and moves its goggling eyes,
The Wax-work, Clock-work, all the marvellous craft
Of modern Merlins, Wild Beasts, Puppet Shows,
All out-o'-the-way, far-fetched, perverted things,
All freaks of nature, all Promethean thoughts
Of man, his dulness, madness, and their feats
All jumbled up together, to compose
A Parliament of Monsters.
· · · · · · · · · · · · · · · ·
    Oh, blank confusion! true epitome
Of what the mighty City is herself,
To thousands upon thousands of her sons,
Living amid the same perpetual whirl
Of trivial objects, melted and reduced
To one identity, by differences
That have no law, no meaning, and no end—
Oppression, under which even highest minds
Must labour, whence the highest are not free.[41]

In this section of *The Prelude,* Wordsworth recalls a visit to the fair
which he made with Lamb in 1802.[42] The picture is bleak—full of
confusion and discord. As Wordsworth points out in lines 731–71,
unless the observer has "an under-sense of greatness" and of "The
Spirit of Nature," the fair is "an unmanageable sight." As often
happens, Wordsworth seems to crystallize some of the unspoken
problems that underlie early nineteenth-century attitudes toward
Jonson. Although Jonson does, in fact, re-create the fair, something which he stresses in his Induction, he never abandons his
view of man as a weak urban creature with innate vices. In *Bartholomew Fair* each character is reminded that he is "but Adam,
flesh and blood." Both the historical fair and Jonson's fair depend
on an audience's sympathy for urban pleasures to achieve an effect.
Wordsworth and the other Romantic critics lack this sympathy,

though they see, quite accurately, that the fair (whether Smithfield's or Jonson's) is a "true epitome" of the city. But this section of *The Prelude* suggests another point: Wordsworth's persona views the fair from "some showman's platform" (685), and his observation focuses on the shows of the fair, its theatricality. What little remained of Renaissance staging in nineteenth-century England survived in the booths of the fairgrounds, and, once again, it was far from congenial to cultured tastes. Moreover, Jonson's play depends on an audience that cares about and for the theater. Certainly it would be both unfair and inaccurate to deny Romantic and Victorian critics any concern for the theater—yet how very different from Jonson's theater was theirs! And one need not read Lamb's essay "On the Tragedies of Shakespeare Considered with Reference to their Fitness for Stage Presentation" in order to recognize the careful distinction made between that which was theatrical and that which was, more importantly, dramatic.

This difference in theatrical presentation made it virtually impossible for Jonson's work to succeed in production, even if it had met with critical praise. (Indeed, given the radical differences, one is surprised that any Renaissance play succeeded on the nineteenth-century stage.) To begin with, the nineteenth-century theaters offered the star system and declamatory acting, both fatal to an ensemble piece like *Bartholomew Fair.* The enormous size of the theaters, the separation of the audience from the stage, and the noisiness of the audience all meant that managers preferred spectacle to risky revivals of Jacobean city comedies. Yet Charles Dickens, so like Jonson in his work, did manage a successful revival of *Every Man in His Humor* in 1845 and again in 1846. One must ask why this play succeeded, given the odds against it or anything else in the Jonson canon.

The primary reason was the unusual set of circumstances surrounding its production.[43] Dickens's company gave avowedly amateur performances, generally to friends, for charity. In this situation they were unlikely to fail. Nor did the performers use Jonson's text, preferring Garrick's adaptation, which was more fitted for their stage. Finally, one might question the actual success. Charles Macready was in Dickens's first-night audience, and although he praised several of the performers "as amateurs," he found the comedy "a very dull business."[44] Another account of the evening comes from Jane Carlyle, who thought the acting was "nothing 'to speak of'": and reported that she had met Tennyson during the interval in "a long dim passage . . . with his head touching the ceiling like a caryatid, to all appearance asleep, or resolutely trying it under most unfavourable circumstances."[45] These sentiments would not have surprised Dickens himself, since he had written to Macready:

> Between you and me, and that Post which is in everybody's confidence, I don't think [Bobadill is] a very good part, and I think the comedy is anything but a very good play. It is such a damned thing to have all the people perpetually coming on to say their part, without any action to bring 'em in, or take 'em out, or keep 'em going.[46]

One can imagine what he would have thought of *Bartholomew Fair* given this last remark, for the heart of Jonson's play is characters wandering through the fairground without warrant. Furthermore, unlike *Every Man in His Humor*, there was no Garrick adaptation of *Bartholomew Fair* to render the wandering more palatable. Because of the critical climate and the conditions of the theater, *Bartholomew Fair* continued to sleep. Thanks to the efforts of critics like Gifford and Lamb, it became possible to discuss Jonson dispassionately, even to praise him, as the Romantic fever cooled.

In 1857, Henry Morley wrote *The Memoirs of Bartholomew Fair*, the first serious study of any great fair. His work enjoyed success and is still the definitive book on Smithfield. In it he wrote at length on Jonson's play, praising it both as a document about the Renaissance fair and as a literary work. What he says is astute:

> Ben Jonson's comedy of Bartholomew Fair, though by no means his greatest work, has among his writings one peculiar distinction. It is the most perfect example of his most peculiar character among the poets of his time, and it may even be said of any time.[47]

In short, it is the most characteristic of Jonson's works, a new and interesting idea. But the important thing about Morley's book was not the praise of Jonson's comedy. It was, instead, the way in which his book changed critical opinion about the play's decorum. Once Morley provided an historical context for the work, critics recognized that the play's coarseness came not from Jonson's imagination, but from his accurate observation.

The Restoration critics had praised the play's verisimilitude, despite Jonson's insistence in the Induction that his picture of the fair was more decorous than the actual fair was. Nineteenth-century critics, blinded by their prejudice against Jonson, would have dismissed Jonson's claim of greater decorum as ingenuous and the Restoration's claim of verisimilitude as naive, preferring instead to believe the work scabrous and offensive. After Morley, however, the critical problem of verisimilitude was once more an open question. Some chose simply to ignore it.

Thus John Addington Symonds's appraisal of Jonson for the *English Worthies* series (1886) is favorable, though his discussion of the plays amounts to little more than a polite plot summary (a fact which says much about the public's familiarity with Jonson).[48] To Algernon Swinburne goes the credit of writing about Jonson's plays well enough to evoke interest rather than stifling it with a blanket of praise, contempt, or squeamishness. Simply put, Swinburne's *Study of Ben Jonson* (1888–89) makes sense to twentieth-century ears. One cannot read Swinburne on Jonson without wanting to read Jonson.

Swinburne takes Jonson seriously and enthusiastically. He is perhaps the first to recognize the paradoxical attitudes critics have always expressed about *Bartholomew Fair*. His comments on the play begin with Gifford when he points up a contradiction in Gifford's evaluation of the play and writes, "Who shall decide when not only do doctors disagree, but the most self-confident of doctors in criticism disagrees with himself to so singular an extent?"[49] Swinburne's own comments on the play suggest that he too has a mixed reaction to it. After complaining that its verisimilitude is too accurate, he goes on to praise its comedy, its construction, and its energy. The single sentence that gives his final opinion is a long balanced one, in which each phrase contradicts another:

> When all is said that can reasonably be said against the too accurate and the too voluminous exposition of vulgar and vicious nature in this enormous and multitudinous pageant—too serious in its satire and too various in its movement for a farce, too farcical in its incidents and too violent in its horseplay for a comedy—the delightful humour of its finer scenes, the wonderful vigour and veracity of the whole, the unsurpassed ingenuity and dexterity of the composition, the energy, harmony and versatility of the action, must be admitted to ensure its place for ever among the minor and coarser masterpieces of comic art.[50]

Obviously Swinburne reacted strongly to *Bartholomew Fair;* just as obviously, he is uncertain what to make of the play. He wants to enjoy it wholeheartedly, but finds its darker side disturbing, although the play's darker moments, its "too serious" satire, are what draw him to the play. In another passage, for example, Swinburne warns readers that those who "turn away . . . in sheer disgust" lose "some of the richest and strongest humours." Moreover, he identifies Busy as the embodiment of "execrable fanaticism" whose "immortal" character "towers above the minor characters."[51] Disgusting, yet rich and strong; immortal, towering, and execrable—these conflicting adjectives clearly indicate the paths which twentieth-century critics have taken in discussing the play.

Swinburne's analysis is handicapped, however, by his insistence on the plays' veracity and his blindness toward theatricality. As his editor, Howard Norland, reminds us:

> Unfortunately, his choice of masters did not include a practical dramatic critic, but that was part of the heritage of the Victorian; and unfortunately, too, the contemporary theater did not interest Swinburne. He flatly rejected both the stock melodrama of his age and the new drama developing from the impetus of Ibsen. . . . Following Shelley, Coleridge, and Lamb, Swinburne responded to plays as poetry rather than drama, and, as a result, his criticism at times suffers from prejudice and myopia.[52]

Because of Swinburne, readers began to study Jonson in a new way, but it took William Poel to restore Jonson and his contemporaries to the stage. I need not labor through Poel's importance; almost single-handed he took Renaissance drama from the library and returned it to the playhouse by insisting on a recreation of Elizabethan stage conditions. While his notions of stage delivery and stage design are arguable, no one can question his remarkable gift for resuscitating dead texts by staging them. Even George Bernard Shaw, no lover of Renaissance drama, praised Poel's productions.[53] (Shaw was a notable admirer; another was Swinburne, who twice contributed prologues to plays Poel put on.)[54] In 1898, early in his career, Poel showed an interest in Jonson by staging *The Sad Shepherd* for the Elizabethan Stage Society. Although he never produced *Bartholomew Fair*, he did produce *The Alchemist* (twice), *The Poetaster* (twice), and *Sejanus*.[55] It is not so important to know that Poel liked Jonson or that he never produced *Bartholomew Fair*. What is important is that he made it possible to revive Elizabethan and Jacobean plays without being thought crackbrained. Once he had broken the ground, it was only a matter of time until *Bartholomew Fair* came to life again.

The first revival of the play in almost two hundred years took place under the sponsorship of the Phoenix Society on June 26, 1921. Allan Wade produced the play (and played the Scrivener) at the New Theatre in Oxford.[56] In program notes, Montague Summers praised the play, calling it a masterpiece and "a supreme effort of Jonson's titanic genius," but other critics showed less enthusiasm. (I discuss the critics' reviews in detail in the next chapter.) While the acting received praise, the play did not suit the reviewers' taste. As the critic for the *Times* wrote, "the 'richest humour' of Mr. Roy Byford [Ursula] is too rich for our stomach. . . ,"[57] echoing Swinburne's remark that "some of the meat is too high and some of the sauces are too rank for any but a very strong digestion." This food image was picked up by Robert Noyes in 1938, fourteen years later:

> Rugged old *Bartholomew Fair* must submit to the weakness of the modern stomach, which no longer craves hot roast pig, but prefers orange juice and toast Melba.[58]

No doubt Noyes was right when he wrote this, but the Second World War changed modern tastes. After its horrors and confusions, audiences turned to the theater for new answers to old questions: is life absurd? do morality and reason have any effect? what is our warrant for what we do? In a recent article, Ejner Jensen argues that a true Elizabethan revival has only been possible since the war. Because of Poel's work and the explosion of Shakespeare criticism, we are able "to see the Elizabethan drama in a richer and more comprehensive way."[59] Furthermore, we find Elizabethan drama accessible because our standards of taste and morality are less conservative that those of the Victorian period. Romanticism has been displaced "by a view of art that we call modern" and contemporary dramatists have changed the way we view a play.[60] In *The Duchess of Malfi,* for example, "the play's horrors, unthinkably excessive to earlier critics, took on new validity to a generation that had witnessed the brutalities of Nazism."[61] Like *The Duchess of Malfi,* Jonson's *Bartholomew Fair* addressed modern concerns. Stomachs were stronger and the play's strength as an ensemble piece was appealing. Since the Second World War, *Bartholomew Fair* has been produced more than fifteen times in England.

## [ 7 ]

# The Rebirth of *Bartholomew Fair*

ONE can understand why *Bartholomew Fair* succeeded in Jonson's own lifetime, yet quickly fell out of favor. Its satire on the Puritans pleased King James and the audience at the Hope Theatre, but currents of public opinion shifted rapidly as the country moved closer to civil war. One can understand the play's revived success during the Restoration and again during the early eighteenth century. *Bartholomew Fair* defended the playhouse, which was under attack again and fit the practical demands of the companies. And certainly one can understand why the play fell into abeyance for two centuries. As the times changed, so did tastes: Jonson's play held little appeal for Romantic audiences; the theaters were at a low point; Jonson himself was out of favor. Just as the play faded, so did the popular fair on which it was based, although the death of the fair took much longer. While the traditional theater was stultified in the nineteenth century, people continued to go to the shows and unsanctioned plays at Smithfield. But how is one to account for the play's success after a two-century hiatus? The critics who saw the 1921 revival were largely negative and, in fact, gave several reasons why the play could *not* succeed in the twentieth century.

Newspaper reviews are risky things on which to evaluate a performance; sadly, they are often all that is left. Journalists have to cover too wide a field, commenting sensibly and cogently on classical revivals and bright-eyed musicals; moreover, conditions of performance vary so greatly that one critic may see an excellent production, while another critic sees the play on a lackluster night.

111

The responses to the Phoenix Society revival offer no exception to the rule of contraries: the Manchester *Guardian* commented that "the vigour of the speech remains everlastingly fresh. It is extremely well-spoken by the cast. . . ," while the *Nation and Athenaeum* complained about "the slurred emphasis, the dropping voice, and the lazy, clipped elocution of our colloquial stage English."[1] Despite inconsistencies such as this, the critics of the Phoenix Society revival offer a high level of agreement—only W. J. Turner wrote a positive review.[2]

The common complaints fall into two categories: the play is a museum piece, and its construction is weak. The first charge is the less serious; indeed it may become the hook on which some critic hangs praise. Thus the *Guardian* reviewer denied that the revival was not worth undertaking: "It emphatically was—but more so perhaps from the point of view of the student of Elizabethan literature than from that of a casual theatre-goer."[3] The *Nation* was less enthusiastic, concluding that, in its own day, *Bartholomew Fair* "must have been only half popular," while the *Times* dismissed the production by saying, "As a 'document' *Bartholomew Fair* is full of interest—but that is another matter."[4] What the *Times* found most important was the weakness of the script:

> [Jonson's characters are] merely personified eccentricities, and they behave so irrationally that we do not care a straw what becomes of any of them. A madman perlustrates the stage, only a little more mad than the others, and, if possible, a little more tedious.[5]

The tediousness of an irrational world is a recurring theme; one critic complained that the performance "dragged heavily," while another insisted that the play was obviously *not* "great literature."[6] Herford and Simpson, though generally sympathetic, sum up the performance:

> The parts of Busy and Cokes were admirably played, and the general level of the acting was high. But there was a certain heaviness of movement, due perhaps to the episodic treatment of the characters; they do not move toward a defined goal as the characters of *The Alchemist* clearly do.[7]

Before World War II, an "irrational" play without a "clearly defined goal" was a failure artistically. *Bartholomew Fair* was not worth bothering about except as a picture of Renaissance English life. Once again, the play was valued for its verisimilitude, despite

Jonson's disclaimers. Critics failed to see the play's strength as an ensemble piece, whether they wrote for the newspapers or, like Noyes or Herford and Simpson, wrote for a scholarly audience. More disturbing is their failure to recognize the play's profundity as it investigates man as spectator or tries to locate the sources of authority. In fact, the play *does* have clearly defined goals, but, until a radical dislocation of values occurred during the 1940s, contemporary critics could not see what Jonson had intended.

Since 1947 *Bartholomew Fair* has had eight amateur and eight professional productions in England. Normally one would pass over the amateur productions to concentrate on the professional ones; in the case of *Bartholomew Fair*, however, the play's popularity as an amateur vehicle suggests some of the reasons for its abrupt revival.

*Bartholomew Fair* has several virtues to recommend it to an amateur group. The first of these is novelty: although written by an important dramatist, the play itself is not so well known as *Volpone* or *The Alchemist*. An amateur group does not want to choose a play that has been "done to death," but neither does it want one too obscure. A second point in *Bartholomew Fair*'s favor is its ensemble form: not only does every member of the company have a part; all have a chance to shine in their roles. This strength for amateur companies is a weakness for professional producers because of the enormous payroll it creates. Aside from the expense of salaries, the play is relatively inexpensive to produce. While a ballroom setting can only be decorated at great expense if it is to look properly elegant, a fairground is supposed to look grubby and its booths slipshod. The visual effect of looking "as dirty as Smithfield, and as stinking every whit" strains no one's resources. Given these attractions, *Bartholomew Fair* has proved popular with amateur groups, and, with a few notable exceptions, such groups have done well with it, often choosing the play for a special production. In 1947, for example, the Marlowe Society of Cambridge decided that "after occupying itself for some years now almost exclusively with Shakespearean plays," it was time to produce some by lesser-known Renaissance playwrights; their first attempt was *Bartholomew Fair*.[8] Six years later the intermittent City of London Festival Players chose the play for performance at the Guildhall in honor of Queen Elizabeth II's coronation. The University of Newcastle-upon-Tyne put on a disastrous *Bartholomew Fair* to open its new University Theatre in 1970. Perhaps the saddest of such special productions was that done by the National Youth Theatre in August, 1981; it was the opening production in what seemed certain to be the company's last season, thanks to government cuts. If nothing else, amateur productions of the play have guaranteed that its lively history continues.

Postwar amateur productions begin with the 1947 Marlowe Society performance, which went generally ignored. The Cambridge *Daily News* did review the production, but levelled the old charge that the play was a museum piece, filled with "one-time topicality."[9] Despite this complaint, the reviewer displayed a new attitude toward the play by praising the company's "commendable spirit of experiment." Certainly, whatever a theatergoer's advance expectations, the play must come as a surprise, whether measured against twentieth-century plays or against Renaissance drama. It was, for Jonson, an experimental piece, and to succeed in the theater, a director must recognize and capitalize on that sense of experiment. The reviewer also comments on the production difficulties and particularly on the central problem that a production must overcome—establishing the play's main character, the fair:

> . . . the producer [must] create a bustling background that suggests the traffic of the fair, but nevertheless does not get between the principals and the audience. This is a difficult task and one was not surprised that it did not always come off.

Perhaps if it had, the reviewer would not have remarked that *Bartholomew Fair* "as a joke seemed over-drawn out, and much ado about so little."

Two amateur productions were received amiably: those by the City of London Festival Players (1953) and the Trinity College, Dublin (1963).[10] Both were straightforward, unpretentious productions which made good use of the play's ensemble form. Because audiences came without grandiose expectations, they were greatly entertained. Arthur Colby Sprague remarks of the Dublin production that "audience and actors were at one in their robust enjoyment."[11]

Two amateur productions were unsuccessful: those by the University Theatre, Newcastle-upon-Tyne in 1970 and the Marlowe Society of Cambridge in 1977 (their second revival of the play). In both cases the companies were plagued with production problems beyond their control. The Newcastle performance was intended to inaugurate the new theater, but building ran behind schedule. As a result, not only was it difficult to rehearse the play adequately, but the first few performances took place only after the Administrative Director obtained a temporary public performance licence—temporary because safety standards in the building had not been met. The student newspaper gives a grim account of the first-night misadventures.

> . . . The first 'First Night' was on Friday when a free house of students and workers were given free drinks and free gingerbreadmen, followed by a three and a half hour marathon version of "Bartholomew Fair."
>
> The second 'First Night' was a little different. Instead of an unseamly [*sic*] rush to the bar, waitresses brought gins to the assembled Professors, Civic dignitaries, and celebrities. . . .
>
> Then followed the first two acts of the play lasting an hour and succeeded by an hour's interval. . . . Acts three and four were discreetly laid aside. The third 'First Night' was on Monday[.] Friday was the first time the cast had been able to go through the play on stage without interruption; the lighting circuits had only been on some hours—and were not all working properly. The echo effect of the cavernous interior is distracting and alienating. And one suspects that the cast have not yet had the chance to come to grips with the psychological effects of the racked auditorium, which by placing the audience above the actors makes it that much harder for them to keep their patrons firmly under their thumbs.[12]

One can only admire the student actors' fortitude in going on.

The problems with which the Marlowe Society contended were not so horrendous, but they must have had some effect.[13] At one point the students wanted to set up stocks outside King's College on a Saturday morning and pelt them with fruit (evidently so that the stocks would look authentically smeared on stage). King's College refused permission. A more serious problem arose three days before the play opened when the R.S.P.C.A. learned that the students planned to use live farm animals to re-create the fairground. The society objected vigorously, so the students had to scrap their plans for the animals on stage. An R.S.P.C.A. inspector was quoted as saying, "A goat and a goose might be all right, but pigs are definitely out," a statement which somehow recalls Rabbi Busy. There were things to praise in the production: the reviewer for the Cambridge *Evening News* was pleased with Nightingale's ballad singing and the fairground setting, which "with all its bustle and bawdiness is magical. . . ."[14] But this same reviewer ultimately gave a negative review, complaining that the play is "boring," its action seems "lifeless," and its plot lacks "dramatic momentum." The complaints echo those made by critics about the 1921 revival, and one might conclude that Jonson's play was simply a weak vehicle, were it not for three successful amateur productions.

The first of these also took place at Cambridge. In 1955 the Amateur Dramatics Club mounted the play, flooding an impressionistic set with crowds of actors. One critic noted that the play was "plotless," but found that the production turned this plotlessness to good effect by presenting it as a "great Hogarthian swirl."[15] Reviews of *Bartholomew Fair* have one common feature: because of the size of the cast, whether the critic likes the play or not, he finds himself praising several individual performances. It is unlikely that all the actors will be bad. Of the outstanding performances in this production, two receive special notice. Robin Chapman's portrayal of the "mooing and pursing and rumbling" Rabbi Busy is compared to Tartuffe, while Jonathan Miller's Troubleall, though incoherent, is "touched with natural brilliance."[16]

Four years later the Oxford Experimental Theatre Club brought a production of *Bartholomew Fair* to Stratford for a week.[17] Performed *al fresco*, the production improved on Jonson's original by subjecting Adam Overdo to two duckings in the Avon, as well as the usual beating and the stocks. Once again, many of the cast were praised—including Dudley Moore who played Nightingale—so many in fact that one can justifiably assume the ensemble acting was particularly successful. More heavily cut than the Cambridge production, this one was also better received. The intelligence of the production was especially highly praised; for example, the Manchester *Guardian* called it a performance "as intelligent and comically bright as a needle."[18]

The third important nonprofessional production was that of the National Youth Theatre at London's Royal Court in 1966, and it shared certain features with the successful Oxford and Cambridge productions.[19] Like them, it relied heavily on horseplay and slapstick to characterize Jonson's gallery of eccentrics; like them, it created an effective fairground atmosphere; and like them, it was praised for its clarity. In addition to the considerable amount of business Jonson built into the play, the actors pelted each other with overripe pears and hurled beer mugs about (one of which flew into the stalls and hit a spectator on the head). The stage was constantly busy with action. In general, the production lends credence to the belief that with *Bartholomew Fair*, nothing succeeds like excess. For example, the *Daily Mail* reviewer commented on Trevor Adams as Cokes:

> Babbling with childish delight, screaming like a thwarted toddler, his genial idiocy is inspired and infectious.

Gwynneth Powell's Ursula also brought praise:

> Massive, greasy, bloodied and baring a revoltingly diseased leg as proudly as a banner, she would delight Joan Littlewood with her grotesque presence and assurance.[20]

Often comedies are hurt by overplaying or too much business. As Charles Shattuck has said about Shakespearean productions:

> When Shakespeare is approached by the "stunts-and-games" method, it is not uncommon to find that the stunts and games are brought off with zest and skill, because they are within reach of the actors' understanding; but that the Shakespeare is ill understood, ineptly performed, and, in consequence, worse than boring.[21]

In the case of *Bartholomew Fair*, however, this seems to be less true, undoubtedly because of the difference in the playwrights' intentions. Judging from reviewers' comments, it is difficult for a company to go too far—though not impossible, as we shall see.

This hyperbolic quality must be added to the list of elements that make the play an especially useful vehicle for nonprofessionals. Young actors are particularly prone to overplay comic roles and *Bartholomew Fair* benefits when they indulge themselves. Thus the *Observer* remarked with some truth of the 1966 National Youth Theatre production that *Bartholomew Fair* is "a play young actors can cope with better than the Shakespearean summits."[22] It does not call for great depth from performers; it does demand enormous energy and exuberance.

In the theater, *Bartholomew Fair* must overwhelm the audience, and the audience must be willing to be overwhelmed by a world of appetite and illogic where authority holds no power. Few audiences before the war would submit themselves to this process. The sixteen productions since the war show that the play has, finally, found its audience. Many of the same features that attracted nonprofessionals to the play have attracted professionals as well: in particular, it can clearly claim a part in the traditional repertoire without being overfamiliar to audiences. Companies with a relatively fixed group of players find its ensemble nature attractive, though the strain of paying thirty actors or more sometimes proves prohibitive. Finally, the play addresses modern concerns more directly than any of Jonson's other plays, save perhaps *The Alchemist* or *Volpone*.

When one turns from amateur to professional productions, however, one learns that inventiveness and exuberance are not enough. The important professional productions have succeeded or failed because of the way they handled setting and space in performance.

The first, and easily the most important, postwar production of the play was the one that George Devine mounted in Edinburgh for the Old Vic in 1950;[23] late in that year the production was revived and moved to London. The next production was done by the Bristol Old Vic in 1966,[24] followed two years later by a performance for Radio 3.[25] Terry Hands directed *Bartholomew Fair* in 1969 for the Royal Shakespeare Company.[26] In the summer of 1976, Richard Eyre directed the Nottingham Players in an Edwardian production.[27] Finally, in 1978 the play received two productions: Peter Barnes's at the Round House[28] and Michael Bogdanov's at the Young Vic.[29]

George Devine is the best director *Bartholomew Fair* has ever found. As his involvement with the Royal Court Theatre shows, he combined a willingness to take risks with imagination and intelligence; moreover, he had a professional's working knowledge about every aspect of theater. His preparation for directing *Bartholomew Fair* began when he and Michel Saint-Denis ran an acting school in which Devine taught the comedy classes, using mask-work and improvisation:

> One of his end-of-training shows was a fairground improvisation combining the comedy and movement classes. It had coconut shies and strongmen, side-shows, tight-rope walkers and jugglers: a mass of activity, all operating to a comic ground-plan involving an acrobat who carried his wife upside down while she played the violin, and a Harlequin figure (Pierre Lefevre) who dived through a window at the climax. In this kind of spectacle, the gymnastic side of *commedia* predominated over the funny noses.[30]

He worked particularly hard to teach his students comic technique and comic business, so they could cover their lack of experience. One of his students was Joan Plowright, who has said, "He'd give you something to fall back on if you'd no idea yourself, a little armoury to prevent total despair."[31] Clearly, when Devine came to *Bartholomew Fair* in 1950, he knew how to fill the stage with the frenzied energy of a fair.

Energy and good will often suffice in amateur productions, but professionals must govern them with greater control. *Bartholomew Fair* with its huge cast offers an exceptionally tricky set of problems to a director. Here, too, Devine was well-prepared. He made up his promptbooks fastidiously, writing in notes on stage business and blocking diagrams at every step of the way. Anyone who has examined promptbooks knows how chaotic they can be; Devine's promptbook for *Bartholomew Fair* would delight the most prissy of handwriting teachers with its neatness and the most demanding of theater historians with its completeness. The prompt-text, based on a cut-down acting version, has further directorial cuts clearly marked, occasional glosses, and a wealth of detail about stage movement and business. Thus a brief exchange may be described in detail. To choose one example out of many, Devine turns Win Littlewit into a groaning rag doll when she has her "fit" of longing for roast pig:

> [Win] *groans. Collapses onto* Lit. *He pushes her back to* Dame P., *who pushes her up again.* Win *finally falls forward.*
>
> Pure.  What *shall* we do? Call our zealous brother Busy hither, for his faithful fortification in this charge of the adversary.
>                                                                 (*Exit* Littlewit)
>         Child, *(groan)* my dear child, you shall eat pig.

The exit of Littlewit is in Jonson's text, but all other stage and delivery directions are Devine's. Devine not only adds business; he also adds emphasis to Purecraft's line, "What *shall* we do?" This passage is cut slightly; as a whole, the text is heavily abridged. Nonetheless, the care that Devine spends on a small moment like this one is repeated again and again. At times this attention to detail worked against Devine as a director, as this anecdote shows.

> In professional rehearsal he would prepare an annotated prompt copy, but without [Michel] Saint-Denis's capacity for getting actors to follow it. [Peter] Duguid recalls such a moment with Roger Livesey when 'George said, "Move over here," and Livesey said, "I think I'd prefer to go over there." There was an almighty pause and George was completely thrown.'[32]

Certainly with a cast as large as the one required for *Bartholomew Fair*, the director could not expect complete obedience to his instructions. However, given the play's enormous size, the director who maintains tight control over the details of performance has an obvious advantage over one who lets the production get away from him. Nor was Devine blind to larger effects. The promptbook also contains carefully drawn sketches: one, which accompanies the moment of Overdo's unmasking in act 5, for example, shows the stage positions for thirty-eight actors. The Old Vic promptbook has more than half a dozen such sketches showing how Devine dispersed his troupe across the stage.

Devine had less control over the stage itself. He staged his production at the Edinburgh Assembly hall and at the postwar Old Vic. Despite the best efforts of Motley, the designers, neither venue was effective, although the production was more successful in London than in Edinburgh. To form a stage in the General Assembly Hall of the Church of Scotland, a facade covered up the chancel. This facade was enlivened by a row of "booths" and a long walkway on which part of the performance took place. At either end of the walkway was a set of stairs which led down to the square thrust stage. The audience sat on three sides of this square watching the action. Exits and entrances were made on the stairways from the facade to the thrust stage. The amount of space available to the actors was enormous. Devine did his best to fill this space by outlining stage business like that used in Win's fit; the space was also filled with Motley's sets and costumes, bright and cheerful, evoking an English fair. The company was divided between experienced actors (such as Roger Livesey as Overdo, Ursula Jeans as his wife, Alec Clunes as Wasp) and Devine's students and talented novices (Richard Pasco as the Bookholder, Peter Duguid as the Scrivener and Haggis, Leo M'Kern as Nightingale). One of England's finest puppeteers, George Speaight, was in charge of Leatherhead's motion. Finally, Devine recognized the problems that the audience would have with Jonson's text and tried to solve them by using a heavily cut text and by substituting euphemisms for the more robust language. ("A turd i' your teeth" becomes "grit i' your teeth"; Whit declares "O bless us and save us" instead of "O Creesh!") But all that was promising—the actors' performances, the sets and costumes, the directorial skill—all was swallowed up by the vastness of the Assembly Hall.

The space in the Hall created a number of problems. To begin with, even though there was a cast of close to forty people, the stage was never crowded, and consequently, Devine was never able to establish a fairground ambiance in keeping with Motley's set. Nor were the actors accustomed to playing on a thrust stage with the audience seated on three sides of the performing area. This problem, certainly, was one over which Devine had more control, though teaching forty actors how to perform on a thrust stage is a formidable task. A third problem was the length of time it took actors to make their exits and their entrances via the stairways between the facade and the stage. This problem slowed the pace of an already lengthy production, which ran nearly four hours even with a heavily cut text. Small wonder that Irving Wardle complained in the *Times:*

> On the platform stage of the Assembly Hall here is all the space that the heart of producer [*sic*] could desire. . . . Alas, all this space becomes an embarrassment. . . . Mr. George Devine does what he can with the means at his disposal. . . . It is nobody's fault that a vital requirement is lacking—the hurly-burly of the fair—and that the long exits and entrances slow the pace almost disastrously.[33]

Yet Wardle still praises parts of the Edinburgh production.

> [The play] still has extraordinary comic force. Words that lie somewhat flatly on the printed page leap into life when they are spoken as admirably as for the most part they are spoken by the Old Vic Company, and so realistically do they strike out an atmosphere of roguery or of folly in a few lines that the want of a story is never noticed.

Wardle's final point is particularly perceptive: *Bartholomew Fair*, because it lacks a protagonist, does lack a story in the accepted sense. This lack need not be a great weakness; one can think of Brecht's *Mahagonny* as another, undeniably great, work which "wants a story." Yet, unlike Wardle, most of the newspaper critics blamed problems on Jonson and his play, rather than the staging of the production. This pattern is usual for professional productions of Jonson. When a production succeeds, critics pronounce themselves surprised at the play's excellence. When a production fails, it is generally supposed to be the fault of Jonson. Wardle's review, his sympathetic appraisal of what Devine was trying to accomplish, suggests that Devine's *Bartholomew Fair* was on the right track with its approach, but staged in the wrong theater. Nor is Wardle alone in his praise. Years after seeing the Edinburgh production, the playwright John Arden wrote that he had the feeling of "having actually *been at a fair* (rather than having seen a play about some fictional people at a fair . . .). There was, in fact, the whole of London, shuffling and prowling about on the big Assembly Hall open stage—and each of them, one way or another as cracked as an old carrot. . . . If I were to write social comedy, Jonson was the man to follow. "[34]

When the play moved into the Old Vic as the third production of the 1950–51 season, the reviews became more favorable. As Wardle wrote, the play seemed "twice as effective as it was in the vasts of the Edinburgh Hall. "[35] Yet the stage area still caused problems. During May 1941, the Old Vic stage had taken a direct hit from a bomb and been completely destroyed. In renovating it after the war, the theater's Board of Governors had Pierre Sonrel design a new forestage. In his biography of Devine, Wardle tempered his enthusiastic review of nearly thirty years before when he discussed the effect of this new stage:

> Perhaps through financial compromise, the new stage did not succeed in delivering the intended knock-out blow to the proscenium. It consisted of three bulging hemispheres approached by forestage doors and steps down to the pit. The hemispheres could be linked up, but the idea was to provide acting areas that could be used remotely from the central platform. This carving up of the space greatly restricted the actors' movement, especially as the stage was built on two levels. Anyone making a sweeping entrance through a forestage door was liable to plunge over the edge and straight down into the pit. Val May says, 'the real flaw in the design was that it pushed the audience back from the action because of the moat. Everybody working on it felt that it didn't really help promote the feeling of contact with the house, which was its main purpose.'[36]

Despite this problem with the stage, which undoubtedly limited the blocking of the play, the production enjoyed far greater success than it had in Edinburgh. To a large extent, Devine was able to work out blocking problems, as the stage diagrams in his promptbook show. Moreover, the London production had a shorter running time, although it still required two ten-minute intervals. What is most important about Devine's production is the way he was able to evoke the fair.

That he was able to do so is clear from what Arden has said. How he did so is laid out in his promptbook. The fair, the play's true protagonist, is characterized by Motley's setting, by charac-

ters' movements, and by trust in Jonson's text. The fantastic setting jammed the back of the stage area with extra booths. In addition to the booths for Ursula, Leatherhead, and Joan Trash,
Motley used at different times a monster show, Puppy's wrestling
booth, a barber shop, a peep show, a tobacco cart with a pipe rack,
and streamers. The setting changed at the back of the stage
throughout the play, while the downstage area was left clear for the
enormous cast's performances. The promptbook specifies much
action. In the setting up of the fair in act 2, for example, Devine
introduces more than a dozen passengers and vendors, each with a
piece of business. After crowding the fairgrounds throughout the
play and having his actors deliver Jonson's lines, cut but largely
undiluted, Devine ends the play and the fair with a brilliant theatrical moment which shows his insight into Jonson's play. He fills the
stage with thirty-eight actors for the final unmasking; Overdo
concludes it by inviting everyone to dinner. The stage empties. The
fair is unpopulated—save for its resident madman, Troubleall, who
stands alone before the booths. In the end, all are forgiven, but
only he has warrant to be at *Bartholomew Fair.*

Although five nonprofessional groups mounted the play in the
fifteen years after the Old Vic productions, the next professional
production did not take place until 1966 at the Bristol Old Vic.
The play opened the fourth season at the Little Theatre there, the
modern playhouse of the Bristol Old Vic Company, rather than
the eighteenth-century main house. The director, Christopher
Denys, did a number of things to make the play more accessible
for his audience. Although his play was done in period, he set it in
Bristol in 1610 rather than in London. This change seems questionable, introducing more confusion than it resolves, but perhaps
it heightened local interest in the play. Like Devine, Denys used a
cut text; unlike Devine, Denys cut heavily enough that he was able
to stage the play in just two acts with only one interval. Production
photographs show a young cast, a profusion of beards, and primi-
tive, almost grotesque, puppets. It was a large cast for the Little
Theatre, twenty-six actors, although Devine had used over forty.
Denys, however, did not have to crowd a large thrust stage as
Devine did in Edinburgh, since the Little Theatre has the normal
proscenium stage. Although the Bristol Old Vic production was
not an important one in terms of influence or innovation, Denys
was able to do what he set out to do—mount a quick-paced,
popular version that was like a documentary about low life. The

reviewer for *Stage* praised Arthur Blake (Busy), Frank Middlemass (Overdo), and Gawn Grainger (Littlewit). Of the play as a whole he wrote:

> An excellent idea in theory. The Christopher Denys production of the Jonson piece presents a fast-moving, boisterous picture of the bawdiness of the Jacobean period, although the final verdict is that it's not quite as hilarious as might be expected.[37]

The innovation would have to come with the Royal Shakespeare Company's production three years later.

In publicity for the Bristol Old Vic production, the 1951 London Old Vic production had been mentioned. Its continuing influence can be seen not only in the descriptions of amateur performances, but also in the 1968 radio version done on Radio 3 when Robert Eddison played Cokes, a role which he had performed for Devine to wide praise. (The adaptation for the radio was done by Raymond Raikes, who somehow managed to cut the play to an hour and a half and to eliminate Quarlous!) But in 1969, Terry Hands freed himself and subsequent productions from Devine's version when he directed the play for the Royal Shakespeare company at the Aldwych. While his version was a failure, and often ill-advised, it paved the way for later productions. Unfortunately, but inevitably, critics insisted on comparing Hands's work with Devine's.

Some comments that Hands made in a preproduction interview provide useful background to the production. He began by calling *Bartholomew Fair* the *King Lear* of comedy.

> It's the most remarkable play I've ever worked on. . . . We're delivering the text as cleanly as possible.
>
> It is almost impossible to read—but it comes to life when you hear it. It's as if Jonson wrote it down as he heard it; it's like a tape recording.
>
> It's the most extraordinary *company* play—like a painting by Pieter Breughel the Elder: an enormous canvas with no particular focus. The triumph of Breughel is that he can hold all this in one painting: the triumph of Jonson is to hold this multiple focus all through the play.
>
> I think it's Jonson's greatest—certainly it's the last of his great plays—and he's crammed into it everything he's done, everything he's heard, everything he's learned.
>
> This was a robust man who wrote a robust play. Everybody is flat out all the way.[38]

Had Hands directed the play in the way he suggested when he talked about it, the production would have been far more successful. He could not, however, achieve his vision of the play, perhaps because Hands was young (only twenty-eight) and had too little rehearsal time.

In the interview, Hands stresses four major points:

1. He is trusting the strength of Jonson's text and "delivering [it] as cleanly as possible."
2. The play's vitality depends on the way in which it records Jonson's experience; "it's like a tape recording."
3. The unity of the play comes from its ensemble form; "It's the most extraordinary *company* play."
4. The play requires enormous energy; "Everybody is flat out all the way."

Yet the promptbook and the reviews suggest that he did not follow these points in his production. What the newspaper critics say may be suspect; the promptbook is unequivocal.

Unfortunately, Mr. Hands has refused me permission to quote from the promptbook. He feels that what was done to the text was wrong and unfair to Jonson's greatest play. I will try to summarize clearly what occurs in the promptbook while respecting Mr. Hands's wishes.

To begin with the clean text. Although Hands made fewer cuts than other producers of *Bartholomew Fair,* the play is, of necessity, heavily cut. The playing time was two hours and thirty-five minutes; with two ten-minute intervals, the evening lasted about three hours. (Uncut, the play would run at least an hour longer.) The text was changed in important ways, however, although it was sometimes changed back. Thus at 1.3.137, Hands took Quarlous's line at Wasp's entrance, "Who is this?" and first added an obscenity, then rethought the line, cut the obscenity, and reduced the speech to two words. In the following scene, Jonson has Quarlous ask if Wasp will "Pull on his [Cokes's] boots, a-mornings, or his stockings"; Hands altered this line to include a scatological query. When Wasp despairs of Cokes, he has a delightful speech in the original text which details what wonders a traveler might find in Cokes's brain. The Royal Shakespeare Company version condensed the speech to a brief exit statement that Wasp was going home.

Textual changes are also made to heighten Puritanical hypocrisy.

Before Busy eats at Ursula's stand, he gives a grace that thanks the Lord for food and directs euphemistic scatological revenge against his enemies. Purecraft is given a prayer at Busy's arrest that parodies the psalms. Neither the grace nor the prayer are in Jonson's text.

One more change deserves note. In 4.3, Grace says her manners shall make her husband a good one, and Quarlous replies, "Would I were put forth to making for you, then." In the Royal Shakespeare Company production, this line turns into twentieth-century slang, and Quarlous propositions Grace.

Now there is nothing wrong with changing Jonson's text in order to clarify it. Every twentieth-century director has altered it. But it does seem peculiar that Hands felt the need to make the play more obscene and the Puritans more hypocritical. Surely no audience could misconstrue Jonson's intentions. Gentility is not the play's outstanding feature. And if a director does make such changes, why claim to have used a clean text?

Reading the promptbook, one also wonders what has become of the "tape recording" of Jonson's experience. The play was not done in period; rather the characters wore an anachronistic melange of costumes. The set sketches include a variety of items: a large mirror, barrels, a deckchair, a wicker armchair, a churn, a tea chest, an abandoned car, a diner, and a cable reel table. The play's viewers were reminded of *Hair*, not of Jonson's London. And surely no one can argue that Jonson's play was a seventeenth-century *Hair* or that Jonson would welcome such anachronisms, without revealing a profound misunderstanding of Jonson's radical conservatism. The play does have meaning for twentieth-century audiences, but not in these terms.

Certainly one would have to agree with Hands that the play depends on high-energy ensemble playing for its success. These are qualities that the prompt book cannot testify about. The critics, however, found the play lacking in both regards. As J. C. Trewin wrote in the Birmingham *Post*, ". . . a combination of Jacobean breadth and modern permissiveness can be exasperatingly blatant. Moreover, in the present revival, the players work away with Jonsonian jests while remaining curiously out of touch with each other."[39] (Trewin seems to have recognized the importance of the production since he reviewed it twice.)[40] A reaction similar to his, though more emphatically negative, came from Frank Marcus in *The Sunday Telegraph:*

. . . The production at the Aldwych is a dreadful mess—not due to carelessness or parsimony, but, on the contrary, due to overelaboration and overinterpretation. . . . [It had] noise instead of volume, activity instead of movement, speed instead of rhythm, words instead of poetry. . . .[41]

These reviews do suggest that Hands misused the ensemble and wasted the energy.

Yet how much can one rely on the reviewers' remarks? (Particularly when a reviewer calls for poetry from a great prose comedy!) As one reads through the press clippings, it seems that something indeterminate about the production antagonized the critics who then lashed out, trying to justify their hostility. At times they are led into curious statements about the play; at other points they violently disagree. Surely ignorance accounts for the critic who identified a quotation from Jonson (which he spells "Johnson") as being "an early fifteenth-century text." But Irving Wardle was not at all ignorant about Jonson or his play, and Wardle claimed in the *Times* that "nowhere did Jonson adhere more firmly to his method of comic 'humours' than in this play," a contention that simply does not fit the facts of Jonson's career.[42] To be sure the characters of *Bartholomew Fair* are not rounded, but neither are they as intensely obsessive as the characters in his early satires are. Wardle also complains that "the fairground setting (by Timothy O'Brien) offers little beyond a row of plastic suckling pigs, and a booth fitted out with bicycle pedals." How can one reconcile this remark with the production photos, the promptbook sketches, or the remark by Felix Barker in the *Evening News* that the production is a "timeless extravaganza"?

The review that Roy Strong wrote for *Queen* is particularly interesting. Strong begins by commenting that Hands's production follows the Royal Shakespeare Company's "policy" of reinterpreting the classical repertoire to fit the concerns of postwar society. Since *Bartholomew Fair* centers on a satire of London society in 1614, he argues, Hands's updating is ludicrous, comparable to producing *Look Back in Anger* for Louis XIV: "It just can never work and screams against the text." Next he complains about the dark, menacing stage set, "akin to the camp-follower murk" of a Brecht play. Visually, the production is repellent, and although the actors do their best, they cannot bring the play to life. At this point in his review, Strong examines the reasons the play fails: either the play is bad, or more likely, the play is too topical, too rooted in Jacobean society, "to be produced today with any real success." A successful production today would demand

> . . . all the apparatus with which a Zeffirelli would envelop it: misty London dawns, the cries of London, the actors in ravishing flower-coloured early Stuart dresses.

In this imaginary Zeffirelli production,

> references to cutpurses, galloway naggs, the vapours, and the mallanders would fall into place in what would be a historical evocation.[43]

There are several inconsistencies in what Strong says. His first two paragraphs condemn the updating of the text and the darkness of the production. But it is unclear that the kind of production he suggests in his third paragraph would make the play more palatable. How *could* "flower-coloured dresses" make "the vapours and the mallanders . . . fall into place"? Further, there is little point in comparing Hands's production with an imaginary one if the play could not "be produced today with any real success." The problem here is not with Strong, a man of intelligence and taste, who is quite obviously sincere in what he says. The problem with this review and with others like it is that Hands *did* succeed in presenting a new, and threatening, view of Jonson's fair.

Strong seems almost to be responding to one of two quotations which Hands chose for his program. Poised above a Ralph Steadman caricature of grotesque pigs at a fun fair are the lines:

> It has not been clear for some centuries whether Britain is a kingdom or a republic and we ought to mark the fact by setting up a Republican Jonson Theatre, to balance the Royal Shakespeare.[44]

(The other quotation on the page is the passage from *Discoveries*— "What petty things they are . . ."—that I discussed in Chapter 1.) The idea of Jonson as a republican playwright has its root in the fact that his comedies were about the middle and lower classes, not the upper class, even when he wrote for King James. This view holds that Jonson is for everyman, about everyman, and Shakespeare is only for the rich court circles.

The notion that Shakespeare is a coterie playwright while Jonson is a man of the people simply does not accord with historical fact, but it did become an accepted idea for the production of *Bartholomew Fair* in the 1970s. In other words, it is a myth about Jonson that has validity in today's theatrical world, if not in the scholar's world, in the same way that myths about Jonson as crabbed pedant had validity in the nineteenth century. To ignore Jonson's court connections may not be accurate, but one cannot deny the force of myth.

Many reviewers, however, disliked the myth. Strong's review offers a case in point; the Zefferelli production he describes is clearly "royal," not "republican." In contrast, one critic who endorsed the myth of Jonson was D. A. N. Jones of *The Listener* who wrote an enthusiastic review of the production.[45] It was he, of course, who was quoted in the program as calling for the "republican" Jonson. The generally poor reviews may be traced in part to dislike of a proletarian reading of Jonson's work, but not entirely. Hands's production was badly flawed, as I have tried to show, both because he needlessly exaggerated the violence and hypocrisy of the text and because he failed to achieve a united production that would carry the views he expressed in his preproduction interview with the *Sunday Telegraph.* Finally, one must note that, although Hands tried to suggest the play's relevance to the working class, he failed. As Wardle wrote in an article about working-class drama in the *Times*, "[in] the Aldwych revival of *Bartholomew Fair*, . . . the need to show people working has been disastrously ignored."[46] Despite its problems, the Royal Shakespeare Company production was an influential one, followed by three more professional productions. Jonson's play was increasingly seen as an attack on middle-class hypocrisy by the working class of the fairground.

This republican vision of *Bartholomew Fair* was considerably toned down in the Nottingham Players' 1976 production. The failure of Hands's version showed that the public was not ready for his radical interpretation; equally, the fact that so experimental and well-publicized a production had been done meant that no producer could be unconscious of it. While Richard Eyre, who directed the Nottingham production, did not imitate Hands in the use of eclectic costumes, he did choose an anachronistic late Victorian setting. Eyre used this setting to underline the conflict between the respectable middle-class fairgoers and the lower-class rogues who run the fair.

In act 1, the play was set in a room in Littlewit's house, a room crowded with the heavy furniture of the period, as well as with the reputable bourgeoisie. As one reviewer remarked:

The opening scene—set in the Littlewits' late Victorian parlor—introduced the terms of the play's major contrasts with the clearest comic skill. A vain John Littlewit whose legal work buys him time for exercises in wit, Quarlous and Winwife as rakehell upper-class soldiers, and a Wasp whose class awareness expresses itself in surly assertiveness—all these prepare the way for Busy and Overdo as authority figures whose reforming zeal blinds them to their own enormities.[47]

Crowding the stage space suggested the claustrophobic middle-class world of the late nineteenth century. In sharp contrast to it, the world of the fair, though equally crowded, was colorful and anarchically free.

In the foyer of the theater was an exhibition of nineteenth-century fairground equipment from Lady Bangor's collection at Wookey Hole in Somerset. The music of a steam organ was piped in over loudspeakers. Signs were everywhere saying things like "Girls, It's a Cinch," "Tunnel of Love," and "Join the Happy Throng." Onstage the heavy furniture gave way to strings of colored lights, a set which included items from Lady Bangor's collection, and a sawdust-covered floor. The reviewers commented on the effectiveness of Pamela Howard's "spectacularly colorful" fairground set. Yet the set was not elaborate. As one reviewer commented:

> The set appeared to be simplicity itself: two booths (Lanthorn's and Ursula's) set at angles to suggest alleys and rows of other such establishments stretching through the dust of Smithfield. Ursula's booth was the focus of the early action as it became a rostrum for Overdo, a gathering place for the Smithfield rogues and whores, and (finally) a microcosm of the fair and its excesses. Lanthorn's display, a wonderful assortment of gimcrack toys, was covered with a portable screen and transformed into the puppet theatre at the play's end.[48]

In this production, as in most twentieth-century productions, the company's setting and use of stage space is a crucial factor in the play's success. The director and designer must work together to evoke a fair, or the play's central conflict, whatever the director thinks it is, will not succeed.

But the setting for the fairground is not enough by itself to make the play succeed. Eyre also drew good performances from his actors. Moreover, his casting took an original approach. The lower-class fairground vendors were played by Ken Campbell (Knockem) and his Road Show comedians whose antics suggested an anarchic freedom in the fair. Furthermore, Eyre included eleven "children of the fair," while Cokes was dressed as a Harrovian schoolboy ninny. Their youthful presence contributed much to the lightheartedness of the production, a significant change from Hands's bleak vision of the play. This change had its greatest effect in the play's final scene.

Recent productions of *Bartholomew Fair* see the play as an attack on middle-class morality. Like Alfred Doolittle, the fairground characters are the undeserving poor, who have the fairgoers at their mercy for a change. When the middle-class fights back, as Busy does when he denounces the puppet show, the attack is refuted and middle-class values stand revealed as hypocrisy. This triumph of the fair over the city may be either dark or joyful: in Nottingham the closing moments almost failed to communicate this movement of power from one group to another, but it ultimately succeeded by turning its focus away from the class struggle to the inevitable triumph of the young. As Ejner Jensen wrote:

> The puppet show (with hand puppets, not marionettes) was uninhibited and frenetic, nearly vulgar enough to suggest that Busy's attack on the players had some merit, and it somehow failed to achieve the point of puppet Dionysius' final refutation of the Puritan position. This final and brilliantly theatrical episode was salvaged, however, by the effective use of Cokes and Wasp as spectators. Cokes was played with irrepressible sophomoric enthusiasm; in his response to the puppet-players he fairly shone with that recognition of the power of art that seems accessible only to the truly naïve. The same transforming power took Wasp beyond the limitations of his defensive self-awareness [of class] and pointed him the way to pleasure.[49]

One of the production photographs makes this same point, equating the fair with the young and the poor, showing their triumph over the stuffy middle-class. While Busy engages in argument with the puppets, he is watched by a trio seated on a large carousel animal. It is a pig, an emblem of the fair; they are Punk Alice, Knockem, and one of the children of the fair. Watching Busy's discomfiture and the puppets' antics, all three are delighted.

In the summer of 1978, both Michael Bogdanov and Peter Barnes decided independently to produce *Bartholomew Fair*. Bogdanov had just taken over the Young Vic Company and he chose to do the play as his first production. Barnes was brought to the Round House Theatre by Thelma Holt; it was the first production staged at the Round House without outside management. Although the two men regard the play very differently, there were some similarities in the circumstances of their productions.

Both productions began inauspiciously. Originally Bogdanov had planned to begin at the Young Vic with *Tommy*, which he had done successfully at Leicester; *Bartholomew Fair* was set for the autumn play. But *Tommy* fell through, as did his second choice, *The Buddy Holly Story. Bartholomew Fair* was moved up for a June production. Perhaps the two musicals he had had to abandon influenced Bogdanov's decision to do Jonson's play as a modern-dress musical. In any case, soon after he arrived, he found himself taking over the administrative management of the theater, conducting skills classes, and directing the play with the help of Associate Directors Jeremy James Taylor and Mel Smith. He had only a month in which to mount the production.

Barnes had rehearsal problems of a different sort during his month of rehearsals. On the first day of rehearsal, Barnes climbed onstage to give notes, stumbled, and fell. An ambulance had to carry him away since he had broken his leg. In three days he was back—in a wheelchair—directing the play.

Not surprisingly, neither director is completely satisfied with his production today; both would like to do the play again. But their productions were important ones, and they provide a good place to end this discussion of the play's changing fortunes. It is, perhaps, unfair to compare the productions since they were completely independent, but such a comparison is inevitable since they were almost simultaneous. Although Bogdanov's was a dark production which emphasized the cynical side of the fair, and Barnes's was a more genial view of the Smithfield world, both encountered similar problems in dealing with the text, both made use of extratextual theatricality, and both, like Hands, saw the play as "republican," not "royal."

The first problem a director faces in dealing with a play as long as *Bartholomew Fair* is what will be cut. Although Bogdanov's version was more heavily cut than Barnes's was (to allow time for the musical numbers he added), the promptbooks show surprising agreement about what scenes need trimming. The Induction, as Jonson wrote it, is left out of both promptbooks, although Bogdanov replaced it with a short scene. In it, Lantern Leatherhead came out, welcomed the audience to the Young Vic, and ripped up a copy of the play, warning any culture-seekers that they would not want that rubbish. With that, the entire company came out and sang an invitation to the fair.

Both productions were cut heavily in act 1, particularly in the section about Cokes's character, and in act 2, although small additions were made to gloss obscure lines. The ballad-singing scenes in 2 were shortened in the Round House production. The Young Vic added a song, "The Louder You Scream, the Faster We Go," to introduce the fair at 2.2 and used a production number with a punk rock setting for the ballad-singing in 3.5. Both productions broke for the interval after act 3. The Young Vic opened act 4 with another song, "Pimps and Pawnbrokers," the lyrics of which were an adaptation of a George Alexander Stevens ballad. Both productions cut the vapors scene substantially, as well as large portions of the puppet play that ends *Bartholomew Fair*. The Young Vic company performed "The Piggy Song" at play's end. Cuts were needed, of course, to bring the play's running time under three hours. The Round House text is the more traditional of the two, much closer to Jonson's original, while the Young Vic text, with its interpolated punk rock songs, suggests a louder, angrier production.

Both directors worked to achieve a sense of extratextual theatricality. Bogdanov used strips of cloth to make the entire theater resemble a circus tent, as well as having preshow action (armwrestling, music, acrobats) in the foyer of the theater and the street in front of it. His extension of the fair seems appropriate, given Cokes's last line, "We'll ha' the rest o' the show at home." Barnes, too, moved the spirit of the fair off the stage and into the audience, although the Round House fair was much more extensive than the preshow action at the Young Vic. Originally Barnes thought of having a small fair that would run concurrently with the play. Then Robin Don, the designer, expanded his idea. Next the Round House staff expanded Don's plans. The fair kept getting bigger and bigger. It included the following:

Lucille and Heidi, fortunetelling pigs
five donkeys and two donkey foals (one born the night of dress
  rehearsal)
a Shetland stallion
a Rhode Island Red cockerel with six hens
three geese
twelve mice for mouse racing
Morris Dancers
Punch and Judy
dice games

jugglers, clowns, and minstrels
vendors and stalls
a surly Shakespeare and his whore.

Virtually every review of the production comments on how much
fun the fair was; some, unkindly, go on to praise the fair at the
expense of the play. Perhaps one reason some reviewers preferred
the fair to the play was that Robin Don's design turned the whole
theater into the fairground, a step that meant taking all the seating
out and putting in fairground benches. An audience sitting on
benches without backs for three hours might well be cross.

Although both directors made similar cuts and both took the fair
to the audience, their visions of the play were very different. For
Bogdanov, *Bartholomew Fair* is a dark play about capitalist corruption. Overdo and Busy represent the pretentious middle-class
imposing morals on society. Thus Bogdanov sees Jonson's play as
the revenge of the repressed—immediately relevant to a modern
audience still dealing with corruption and censorship. When we
talked about his production, Mary Whitehouse had just brought a
public indecency suit against him for directing Howard Brenton's
*The Romans in Britain.* He compared the lawsuit to Busy in Jonson's play; as he told me, "It's the same thing happening now."

But one of the production's weaknesses was the gap between the
world Jonson created and "what's happening now." The rewritten
induction, in which Lantern Leatherhead in modern dress spoke to
the audience in colloquial terms, was followed by a burst of punk
rock. After this opening, the plunge into the language of Jonson's
punk jarred:

> The briskness, the point and precision of Jonson's language and obser-
> vation of character are a shock after the slack colloquialism and limp
> tricks of what has gone before.[50]

Bogdanov wanted to use the play on the meaning of "punk" and
the modern dress to make the play "more accessible" to his audience. Today he is less sure about his decision, saying it was not
very successful.

The first three acts, evoking the seamy side of the fair, used
much physical action. Unicycles wove through the fair, acrobats
bounced on a mini-trampoline, the characters ran about and
fought. Through it all moved Adam Overdo (Bill Wallis), innocent, disguised, and genial. But the action, though it kept the play

moving, seemed to be at odds with the text. In the second half, the action and the text finally meshed into a coherent vision during the puppet play.

The second half began with a cynical song, "Pimps and Pawnbrokers," inviting the audience back to the fair. Not only did this song contrast with the play's opening number—"Come to Bartholomew Fair, buy any pears"—it also provided a background to the pursuit and capture of Adam Overdo, who was led to the stocks. The lighthearted quality of the first half faded as Troubleall made his first appearance, the drinkers played their game of vapors, and Knockem recruited Win Littlewit and Alice Overdo as prostitutes. The action converged on the puppet play, a reenactment of the wooing of Grace Wellborn. In this version the puppets took on the roles of the characters in the play: Leander was Cokes; old Cole, Wasp; Hero, Grace; Pythias, Quarlous; Damon, Winwife. Controlling the lot, quarreling with and defeating Busy was Dionysius/Leatherhead, whom Bogdanov thinks of as "the voice of the anarchist, the libertine" and the informing spirit of the play. Just when the complete freedom of the fair seemed assured by Busy's shouting "On with the play," Overdo revealed himself.

His triumph was short-lived, of course, as he soon found his wife among the sinners. In Bogdanov's production, his discovery and shock were heightened when Alice vomited at great length. With revelation came a collapse of the triumph; no one learning the truth was pleased by it, and only Overdo's invitation to dinner made the denouement comic.

Barnes's production was a much more kindly one. To him, those who see bitterness and cynicism in the play are mistaken in their perceptions because they lack familiarity with the fairground world. He does not. His parents ran stalls for vacationers in Clacton-on-Sea; so the approach of tourists, and their money, is something he sees in familiar terms. The situation is not simply a mercenary one for the fairground people; they see a different reality from the holiday crowd.

This is not to imply that Barnes sees the play or Jonson in simple terms. As Irving Wardle remarked:

> I imagine that [*Bartholomew Fair*] must be a text particularly close to Mr. Barnes's heart as it so insistently drives in the message of his own plays, the folly of anyone having power over anyone else.[51]

Barnes regards *Bartholomew Fair* as a play about class struggle and

Jonson as one of the great playwrights of the middle and lower classes. He echoes the statement that we need a republican theater of Jonson as well as a royal theater of Shakespeare. In his eyes, the play concerns metamorphosis—the middle-class visitors to the fair pass through the fair as through a trial and in the process the characters, particularly the Puritans, change their natures. The fair becomes a means of reconciling the classes; it brings together disparate elements of society and releases them to dinner, a feast in the house of authority.

But the house of authority was never seen in the Round House. Barnes extended the fair spatially, from the stage into the auditorium, as well as chronologically, using actors in Jacobean costumes and pieces of nineteenth-century fairground equipment from Lady Bangor's collection to appeal to a twentieth-century audience. The audience in the theater became fairgoers as well, caught up in the business of the fair and changed by their experience of it. Robin Don's set, which permitted the actors to play three-quarters in the round, heightened the immediacy of the fair in a theater as large as the Round House.

One problem with the size of the playing area, however, was the pace. The complexity of the plot also created problems which demanded fast action on stage. In a rehearsal diary kept by Michael Gearin-Tosh, there is the comment that "the plot is so complicated that the audience will only remember who characters are if they reappear quickly. Everything must be a mad rush." In performance the actors were able to achieve the fast pace, but this created a new problem. How was Barnes to make the actors appear human, rather than robot-like creatures who scurried on and off?

Barnes and his actors worked to accomplish this by making the characters more sympathetic than they are usually played. In the case of Wasp, bad-tempered and inconsistent, Henry Woolf, who had the role, tried to play the character as a batman with a dull officer cadet rather than as a tutor with a half-witted pupil. Peter Bayliss, playing Adam Overdo, confided his soliloquies to the audience instead of declaiming them. The general shift in characters, the metamorphosis worked by the fair, made the fairground world gradually seem to be the sane one, while the visitors became progressively more grotesque. One result of this strategy was that the real madman, Troubleall (David Claridge), stood out amongst the antics of the fairground by being more serious than anyone else. Thus even when Troubleall tells Cokes (John Wells) that he must have Overdo's warrant, the madman took Cokes's hand and patted it. As Wardle commented, Troubleall's "monotonous demands are underscored with a changing sub-text of kindness, fear, and bewilderment."[52]

This gentle madman disappears for most of the puppet play, of course, since Quarlous has stolen his breeches. Using lifesized puppets, the company played the final scene as knockabout farce. The ugly moments of the scene were played down. Indeed the last few lines of the production are largely Barnes's interpolations. He cut some of Overdo's final didactic speech, replacing it with lines for Busy, Wasp, and Ursula:

| | |
|---|---|
| *Overdo.* | I invite you home with me to my house, for supper. |
| *Busy* | Will there be roast pig? |
| *Overdo.* | Yes, and I will have none fear to come along, for my intents are "ad aedificandum, non ad diruendum." |
| *Wasp.* | He means to "build up, not tear down." |
| *Overdo.* | So lead on. |
| *Ursula.* | To supper! |
| *Cokes.* | Yes, and bring the rest of the actors along, we'll ha' the rest o' the play at home. |

The business of the fair is over. But, as the fairgoers depart, taking their money with them, the fair springs to life again in the house of authority.

In the twentieth century there has been a tendency to regard *Bartholomew Fair* either as dark and cynical (Hands's and Bogdanov's productions) or as genial (Devine's and Barnes's). Obviously how one understands the play and Jonson's intentions will determine whose production one likes best. Thus one reviewer dismissed the Round House version as "a nice, clean, safe, bright, sweet Jacobean panto," while Wardle said of it:

> I do not wish to belittle the other recent versions at Nottingham and the Young Vic, but this is the first time I feel I have really seen the play.[53]

To compare the productions further would be foolish, especially since each was, in its own way, successful. *Bartholomew Fair* has always been a play which reflected its audiences. No doubt the Hope Theatre audience thought Jonson wrote especially for them, while King James and his court delighted in all the allusions that showed that Jonson kept them in mind as he wrote. If we can go by

Pepys's diary entries, the Restoration audience found the play an accurate reflection of their own continuing disputes with the Puritan faction. Later in the eighteenth century, it became a play peculiarly suited to the needs of the company at Drury Lane and one that effectively answered the charges of Jeremy Collier. The later eighteenth century and the nineteenth century repudiated the truths Jonson told them about corruption and city life; to their eyes, the play's reflection was a grotesque distortion. In the twentieth century the play once again tells us what we want to hear. Its renewed popularity, particularly with younger audiences, rests in its relevance to our concerns with class and with morality. Fairgrounds have not changed much in three or four centuries. Until they do, *Bartholomew Fair* will live on.

# Appendix A:
# Casting of *Bartholomew Fair* in the 18th Century

| | | | | Character | | | |
|---|---|---|---|---|---|---|---|
| Date | Cokes | Overdo | Quarlous | Winwife | Edgworth | Wasp | Littlewit |
| 8-12-1707 | Bullock | Keen | Mills | Husband | Booth | Johnson | Norris |
| 8-14-1707 | Bullock | Keen | Mills | Husband | Booth | Johnson | Norris |
| 8-22-1707 | Bullock | Keen | Mills | Husband | Booth | Johnson | Norris |
| 10-22-1707 | Bullock | Keen | Mills | Husband | Booth | Johnson | Norris |
| 7-15-1708 | Bullock | Keen | Mills | Bickerstaff | Booth | Johnson | Norris |
| 8-31-1708 | Bullock | Keen | Powell | Husband | Thurmond, Jr. | Johnson | Norris |
| 6-1-1710 | Bullock | — | Mills | Husband | — | Johnson | Bowen |
| 3-8-1711 | Bullock, Sr. | — | Mills | Husband | Bullock, Jr. | Johnson | Norris |
| 8-24-1711 | Bullock, Sr. | — | Mills | Elrington | Bullock, Jr. | Johnson | Norris |
| 8-26-1712 | Bullock, Sr. | — | Mills | — | — | Johnson | Norris |
| 1-14-1713 | Bullock, Sr. | — | Mills | — | Bullock, Jr. | Johnson | Norris |
| 6-28-1715 | Miller | Shepherd | Mills | Quin | Ryan | Johnson | Norris |
| 7-16-1717 | Miller? | — | Mills? | Quin? | Ryan? | Johnson? | Norris? |
| 3-24-1718 | Miller | — | Mills | — | — | Johnson | Norris |
| 6-27-1718 | Miller? | — | Mills? | Wilks? | Walker? | Johnson? | Norris? |
| 11-26-1718 | Miller | — | Mills | — | — | Johnson | Norris |
| 8-4-1719 | Miller | — | Mills | — | — | Johnson | Norris |
| 1-13-1720 | Miller | Shepard | Mills | Wilks, Jr. | Walker | Johnson | Norris |
| 6-10-1720 | Miller | Shepard | Mills | Wilks, Jr. | Walker | Johnson | Norris |
| 10-30-1731 | Cibber, Jr. | Shepard | W. Mills | Watson | A. Hallam | Johnson | Oates |
| 8-25-1735 | Mullart | Lacy | — | — | — | Jones | — |

—denotes actor unknown; ? indicates role assignment is questionable.

No cast lines for 8-26-1708, 12-1-1713, 12-10-1716, 4-28-1719, 10-31-1720, 7-10-1722, and 12-21-1722.

Other role assignments: 7-15-1708, Mrs. Winwife by Mrs. Saunders. 8-31-1708, Crumplin by Leigh, Leatherhead by Carnaby. 10-30-1731, Leatherhead by R. Wetherilt, Trash by Wright. 8-25-1735, Ananias by Aston, Constable by Littleton, Florella by Miss Brett, Loveit by Mrs. Mullart, Nutwoman by Mrs. Brunnette, Pickle Herring by Mrs. Charke, Rover by Boothby, Silence by Turner, Toyman by Topham, Trash by Mrs. Mann, Valentine by Mrs. Talbot, and Watchman by Machen.

| | | | Character | | | |
|---|---|---|---|---|---|---|
| Busy | Ursula | Nightingale | Grace | Purecraft | Win | Mrs. Overdo |
| Pack | Mr. Cross | Fairbank | Mrs. Porter | Mrs. Powell | — | — |
| Pack | Mr. Cross | Fairbank | Mrs. Porter | Mrs. Powell | — | — |
| Pack | Mr. Cross | Fairbank | Mrs. Porter | Mrs. Powell | — | — |
| Cibber | Mrs. Cross? | Fairbank | Mrs. Bradshaw | Mrs. Powell | Mrs. Saunders | — |
| Pack | Mrs. Cross? | Fairbank | Mrs. Moor | Mrs. Powell | —? | Mrs. Mills |
| Bickerstaff | Mr. Cross | Fairbank | Mrs. Moor | Mrs. Powell | Mrs. Saunders | Mrs. Cox |
| Cibber | — | Bowman | Miss Willis | Mrs. Powell | Mrs. Saunders | — |
| Cibber | — | — | Miss Willis | — | Mrs. Saunders | — |
| Pack | Mr. Cross | Burkhead | Miss Willis | Mrs. Powell | Mrs. Saunders | — |
| Pack | — | — | — | — | Mrs. Saunders | — |
| Pack | — | — | Miss Willis | — | Mrs. Saunders | — |
| Bickerstaff | Mr. Cross | Birkhead? | Miss Willis | — | Mrs. Saunders | — |
| Bickerstaff? | Mr. Cross? | — | — | — | — | — |
| Cibber | F. Leigh | — | Miss Willis | — | Mrs. Saunders | — |
| Bickerstaff | — | — | — | — | — | — |
| Cibber | — | — | Miss Willis | — | Mrs. Saunders | — |
| Bickerstaff | — | — | — | — | — | — |
| Bickerstaff | Cross | — | — | Mrs. Baker | Mrs. Saunders | Mrs. Moor |
| Bickerstaff | Cross | — | — | Mrs. Baker | Mrs. Saunders | Mrs. Moor |
| Griffin | Harper | Stoppelaer | Mrs. Butler | Mrs. Wetherilt | Mrs. Raftor (Kitty Clive) | Mrs. Shireburn |
| — | — | — | — | — | — | Miss Bennet |

# Appendix B: Casting in 20th-Century Professional Productions

Old Vic at the Edinburgh International Festival of Music and Drama, August 1950

| | | |
|---|---|---|
| *Induction* | Stage-keeper | Paul Rogers |
| | Bookholder | Richard Pasco |
| | Scrivener | Peter Duguid |
| | | |
| *Play* | Littlewit | Anthony Van Bridge |
| | Win Littlewit | Dorothy Tutin |
| | Winwife | John Van Eyssen |
| | Quarlous | Esmond Knight |
| | Wasp | Alec Clunes |
| | Cokes | Robert Eddison |
| | Dame Overdo | Ursula Jeans |
| | Grace | Heather Stannard |
| | Purecraft | Dorothy Green |
| | Busy | Mark Dignam |
| | Overdo | Roger Livesey |
| | Lantern Leatherhead | Pierre Lefevre |
| | Joan Trash | Sheila Ballantine |
| | Nightingale | Leo M'Kern |
| | Ursula | Nuna Davey |
| | Mooncalf | Brian Smith |
| | Knockem | William Devlin |
| | Edgeworth | Paul Hansard |
| | Costardmonger | Lee Montague |
| | Corncutter | Leonard Maley |
| | Mousetrap Man | James Grout |

| | |
|---|---|
| Whit | Douglas Wilmer |
| Bristle | Rupert Davies |
| Haggis | Peter Duguid |
| Trouble-All | Paul Rogers |
| Val Cutting | James Grout |
| Northern | James Wellman |
| Puppy | Richard Walter |
| Filcher | James Wellman |
| Sharkwell | Richard Walter |
| Puppeteers | George Speaight |
| | Leonard Maley |

Producer: George Devine; Scenery/Costumes: MOTLEY; Puppets: George Speaight; Music: arranger Jani Strausser; Lighting: Cecil Clarke

Visitors to the Fair, Stallholders, Watchmen: Jan Bashford, Christopher Burgess, Jean Cooke, Sheila Cooper, Patience Gee, Joan Poulter, Elizabeth Rogers, Pamela Wickington, Mary Wylie, Bernard Kay, Michael Keir, Leonard Maley, Rex Robinson

## Old Vic at the Old Vic Theatre, London, December 1950

The cast was as for Edinburgh with the following changes:

| | |
|---|---|
| Winwife | John Ebdon |
| Quarlous | Douglas Wilmer |
| Grace | Pauline Jameson |
| Whit | John Blatchley |
| Barber | George Speaight |
| Watchmen | Leonard Maley |
| | Bernard Kaye |
| | Rex Robinson |

Orchestra director: Harold Ingram; Fights: arranger Charles Alexis

## The Bristol Old Vic at the Little Theatre, Bristol, August 1966

| | |
|---|---|
| Littlewit | Gawn Grainger |
| Win Littlewit | Pamela Buckle |
| Winwife | Stephen Fagan |
| Quarlous | Matthew Roberton |
| Wasp | John White |
| Cokes | Christopher Serle |

| | |
|---|---|
| Dame Overdo | Marjorie Yates |
| Grace | Joan Morrow |
| Purecraft | Julia McCarthy |
| Busy | Arthur Blake |
| Overdo | Frank Middlemass |
| Lantern Leatherhead | Garry Files |
| Trash | Janet Key |
| Ursula | Claire Davenport |
| Mooncalf | Charles McKeown |
| Wit [sic] | Desmond Stokes |
| Knockem | Roger Bizley |
| Edgworth | Colin McCormack |
| Bristle | Gabriel Prendergast |
| Haggis | Richard Glyn Lewis |
| Troubleall | Charles McKeown |
| Alice | Janet Key |
| Costardmonger | Richard Glyn Lewis |
| Val Cutting | Philip Taylor |
| Porters/Puppeteers | Michael Grensted |
| | Sally Barling |

Director: Christopher Denys; designers: Graham Barlow, Michael Swindlehurst

### Radio 3, July 7, 1968

| | |
|---|---|
| Stagekeeper | Ian Thompson |
| Bookholder | Peter Baldwin |
| Littlewit | David Brierly |
| Win | Carol Marsh |
| Winwife | Denys Hawthorne |
| Wasp | Carleton Hobbs |
| Cokes | Robert Eddison |
| Grace | Rosalind Shanks |
| Dame Overdo | Betty Handy |
| Purecraft | Elizabeth Morgan |
| Busy | Charles Gray |
| Leatherhead | Ronald Herdman |
| Trash | Barbara Mitchell |
| Nightingale | Alan Dudley |
| Costardmonger | Peter Baldwin |
| Overdo | John Justin |
| Ursula | Norah Blaney |
| Mooncalf | Geoffrey Wincott |
| Knockem | Francis de Wolff |
| Edgworth | Anthony Jackson |

| Haggis | Duncan McIntyre |
|---|---|
| Bristle | Ian Thompson |
| Punk Alice | Elizabeth Morgan |
| Filcher | Antony Viccars |
| Sharkwell | Christopher Bidmead |

Adapted and produced by Raymond Raikes

The Royal Shakespeare Company at the Aldwych Theatre, London, October 1968

*Induction*

| Stage Keeper | John Kane |
|---|---|
| Book Holder | Richard Jones Barry |
| Scrivener | Julian Curry |

*At John Littlewit's*

| Littlewit | Terence Hardiman |
|---|---|
| Win | Helen Mirren |
| Purecraft | Patience Collier |
| Busy | Willoughby Goddard |
| Winwife | Ben Kingsley |
| Quarlous | Norman Rodway |
| Cokes | Alan Howard |
| Wasp | Clifford Rose |
| Dame Overdo | Hildegard Neil |
| Grace | Domini Blythe |

*Near the Fair*

| Overdo | Sebastian Shaw |
|---|---|

*At the Fair*

| Leatherhead | Patrick Stewart |
|---|---|
| Trash | Ruby Head |
| Filcher | Glynne Lewis |
| Sharkwell | Robert Oates |
| Ursula | Lila Kaye |
| Mooncalf | Ralph Cotterill |
| Knockem | Richard Moore |
| Whit | Bruce Myers |
| Cutting | Julian Curry |
| Alice | Mary Rutherford |
| Edgworth | John Kane |
| Nightingale | Bernard Lloyd |

| | |
|---|---|
| Trouble-All | Phillip Manikum |
| Bristle | Ted Valentine |
| Haggise [*sic*] | George Cormack |
| Pocher [*sic*] | Richard Jones Barry |
| Puppy | Hugh Keays Byrne |
| Nordern | Ian Dyson |
| Costardmonger | John York |
| Corncutter | David Stern |
| Mousetrap-man | David Sadgrove |
| Fortune-teller | Valerie Minifie |
| Passenger | Paul Arlington |
| Youth | Martin Bax |
| Cripple | Peter Cochran |
| Porter | David Forbes |
| Blind Man | Peter Harlowe |
| Drunk | Stephen Turner |
| Children | David Papworth |
| | Stephen Papworth |
| | Paul Swift |

*The Puppet Play*

| | |
|---|---|
| Hero | Valerie Minifie/Mary Rutherford |
| Leander | Martin Bax/Richard Jones Barry |
| Damon | Peter Harlow/Ian Dyson |
| Pythias | Paul Arlington/Robert Oates |
| Cupid | David Forbes/Hugh Keays Byrne |
| Cole | Peter Cochran/David Sadgrove |
| Dionysius | Stephen Turner/David Stern/Julian Curry |

Director: Terry Hands; Designer: Timothy O'Brien; Music: Guy Woolfenden; Puppet advisor: Barry Smith

---

Nottingham Players at the Nottingham Playhouse, June 1976

| | |
|---|---|
| Littlewit | Roger Booth |
| Win | Judy Liebert |
| Purecraft | Pat Keen |
| Busy | Malcolm Storry |
| Winwife | Chris Langham |
| Quarlous | John Dicks |
| | |
| Cokes | David Beames |
| Wasp | Matthew Scurfield |

| | |
|---|---|
| Grace | Celia Foxe |
| Adam Overdo | Roger Hume |
| Dame Overdo | Grania Hayes |
| | |
| Lanthorn Leatherhead | Ted Richards |
| Joan Trash | Carolyn Pickles |
| Edgworth | Sylveste McCoy |
| Nightingale | Andy Andrews |
| Knockem | Ken Campbell |
| Whit | Eugene Geasley |
| Ursula | Arthur Kohn |
| Mooncalf | Chris Lillicrap |
| | |
| Troubleall | Ralph Nossek |
| | |
| Bristle | Duncan Faber |
| Haggis | Nigel Bennett |
| Filcher | Kostakis Theodossiou |
| Northern | Nigel Bennett |
| Alice | Judy Riley |
| Costermonger | Kostakis Theodossiou |
| Whores | Jane Gurnett |
| | Julia Watson |

Children of the Fair: Matthew Bates, Justice Butler, Adam Crevald, Andrew Crevald, Andrew Dixon, Peter Mersereau, Stephen Mersereau, Barnaby Pitt, Miranda Pitt, Ben Silburn, Luke Silburn

| | |
|---|---|
| Puppet Master | Barry Smith |
| Puppet Operators | Duncan Faber |
| | Chris Lillicrap |
| | Sylveste McCoy |

Director: Richard Eyre; Designer: Pamela Howard; Lighting: Geoffrey Mersereau; Assistant Director: Richard H. Williams

The Young Vic at the Young Vic Theatre, London, June 1978

| | |
|---|---|
| John Littlewit | Michael Attwell |
| Win Littlewit | Penelope Nice |
| Dame Purecraft | Kate Versey |
| Zeal of the Land Busy | Malcolm Rennie |
| Dame Alice Overdo | Tina Jones |
| Grace Wellborn | Fiona Victory |

| | |
|---|---|
| Bartholomew Cokes | Philip Bowen |
| Humphry Wasp | Tim Thomas |
| Ned Winwife | Frederick Warder |
| Tom Quarlous | John Labanowski |
| Adam Overdo | Bill Wallis |

*Characters of the Fair*

| | |
|---|---|
| Ursula | Laura Cox |
| Mooncalf | Chris Barnes |
| Lanthorn Leatherhead | James Carter |
| Jordan Knockem | Micky O'Donoughue |
| Captain Whit | Terry Mortimer |
| Nightingale | Joss Buckley |
| Ezekial Edgworth | Stephen Boxer |
| Joan Trash | Heather Baskerville |
| Troubleall | Bev Willis |
| Davy Bristle | Christopher Ashley |

Other parts played by members of the company.

Director: Michael Bogdanov; Assistant Directors: Jeremy James Taylor, Mel Smith; Designer: Paul Bannister; Lighting: Michael Alvey; Production Manager: Richard Bullimore; Puppets: Richard Dean, Stefan Baran

Music and Lyrics by the Young Vic Company

The Round House Trust at the Round House Theatre, London, August 1978

| | |
|---|---|
| John Littlewit | Jonathan Cecil |
| Win Littlewit | Victoria Plucknett |
| Dame Purecraft | Sheila Burrell |
| Zeal-of-the-Land Busy | Rowland Davies |
| Winwife | Maurice Colbourne |
| Quarlous | Donald Gee |
| Bartholomew Cokes | John Wells |
| Humphrey Wasp | Henry Woolf |
| Adam Overdo | Peter Bayliss |
| Dame Overdo | Iona Banks |
| Grace Wellborn | Jennie Stoller |
| Lantern Leatherhead | Antony Milner |
| Joan Trash | Patricia Ford |
| Ezekial Edgworth | Steven Beard |
| Nightingale | David Foxxe |
| Ursula | Fanny Carby |

| | |
|---|---|
| Mooncalf | Peter Craze |
| Jordan Knockem | David Bailie |
| Captain Whit | Peter Craze |
| Punk Alice | Patricia Ford |
| Trouble-All | David Claridge |
| Haggis | David Foxxe |
| Bristle | Marcus Bell |
| Filcher | Patricia Ford |
| Sharkwell | Marcus Bell |

Director: Peter Barnes; Designer: Robin Don with Tanya McCallin; Music: John Riley; Costumes: Lindy Hemming; Animals: Michael Hirst; Puppets: David Claridge

# Notes

### Chapter 1. Smithfield and Jonson

1. E. B. Partridge, "Jonson's Large and Unique View of Life," in *Elizabethan Theatre,* vol. 4, ed. G. R. Hibbard (London: Macmillian, 1974), 147–48.

2. T. S. Eliot, *Selected Essays, 1917–1932* (New York: Harcourt, Brace and Company, 1932), 274.

3. John S. Weld, "Christian Comedy: *Volpone,*" *Studies in Philology* 51 (1954): 172–93; Jackson Cope, "*Bartholomew Fair* as Blasphemy," *Renaissance Drama* 8 (1965): 127–52; Robert Knoll, *Ben Jonson's Plays: An Introduction* (Lincoln: University of Nebraska Press, 1964), 105.

4. The collection of comments is taken (rather unfairly) from the following works:

(a) E. A. Horsman, ed., *The Revels Plays: Bartholomew Fair* (Cambridge, Mass.: Harvard University Press, 1960), xiii.

(b) Alan Dessen, *Jonson's Moral Comedy* (Evanston: Northwestern University Press, 1971), 218.

(c) C. H. Herford, Percy Simpson and Evelyn Simpson, *Ben Jonson* (Oxford: Clarendon Press, 1925–52), 2:145.

(d) Freda L. Townsend, *Apologie for Bartholomew Fayre* (New York: Modern Language Association, 1947), 71.

(e) Jonas Barish, *Ben Jonson and the Language of Prose Comedy* (Cambridge, Mass.: Harvard University Press, 1960), 222.

(f) William D. Wolf, *Jacobean Drama Studies: The Reform of the Fallen World* (Salzburg: Salzburg Studies in English Literature, 1973), 115.

(g) John J. Enck, *Jonson and the Comic Truth* (Madison: University of Wisconsin Press, 1966), 198.

(h) Jackson Cope, "*Bartholomew Fair* as Blasphemy," *Renaissance Drama* 8 (1965): 144.

(i) C. G. Thayer, *Ben Jonson: Studies in the Plays* (Norman: University of Oklahoma Press, 1963), 132–33.

(j) L. A. Beaurline, *Jonson and Elizabethan Comedy* (San Marino: Huntington Library, 1978), 236.

(k) Edmund Wilson, "Morose Ben Jonson," in *Ben Jonson,* ed. Jonas Barish (Englewood Cliffs, N.J.: Prentice-Hall, 1963), 63. Hereafter cited as *Twentieth Century Views.*

(l) Gabrielle Jackson, *Vision and Judgment in Ben Jonson's Drama* (New Haven: Yale University Press, 1968), 73.

(m) Algernon Charles Swinburne, *A Study of Ben Jonson*, ed. Howard B. Norland (1889; reprint, Lincoln: University of Nebraska Press, 1969), 61.

(n) Eugene M. Waith, ed., *The Yale Ben Jonson: Bartholomew Fair* (New Haven: Yale University Press, 1963), 15.

5. Herford and Simpson, 10:181 for *Bartholomew Fair;* 10:14 for *Epicoene*. In the notes, Herford and Simpson will be referred to as H&S; quotations from the play will be taken from the Yale edition edited by Eugene Waith (New Haven, 1963).

6. H&S, 10:185.

7. The information on Rahere's life and reputation is taken from the entry in the *Dictionary of National Biography* and from Henry Morley's *Memoirs of Bartholomew Fair* (London: Frederick Warne, 1859).

8. Quoted in Morley, 2.

9. *DNB* specifies the disease.

10. Jonson makes the same accusation against Puritans in *The Alchemist*, 1.1.128.

11. Morley, 22ff.

12. Morley, 8–10; 23–24; the miracle of the missing book is described on 8.

13. Morley, 26.

14. Bil Baird, *The Art of the Puppet* (New York: Ridge Press, 1973), 67. For the religious beginnings of English puppet plays, see E. K. Chambers, *Mediaeval Stage* (Oxford: The University Press, 1903), 2:159ff.

15. Baird, 69. In a list of puppet plays performed in England, George Speaight mentions fourteen which are known to have been produced before 1614. *The History of the English Puppet Theatre* (New York: John de Graff, n.d.), 324–43.

16. *The Dramatic Works of Thomas Dekker*, ed. Fredson Bowers (Cambridge: The University Press, 1953), 1:364.

17. Dekker, 325.

18. Reproduced in Morley, 68; cf. 64, 70 for similar illustrations of scenes from miracle plays.

19. Morley, 65–66, says the performance for Richard II took place in 1390; Chambers, 2:118–19, says 1391.

20. Morley gives the text of the Lord Mayor's 1604 proclamation which calls for wrestling, 110.12.

21. Morley, 77.

22. Morley, 78–79.

23. Edward B. Partridge, ed., *Bartholomew Fair* (Lincoln: University of Nebraska Press, 1964), x.

24. Morley, 86–93.

25. My account of the Saint Bartholomew's Day Massacre is drawn from Will and Ariel Durant's *The Age of Reason Begins* (New York: Simon and Schuster, 1961), 346ff. and J. E. Neale, *Queen Elizabeth I* (New York: Doubleday Anchor, 1957), 229ff.

26. Morley, 104.

27. As Margot Heinemann has pointed out, Jonson disliked venality in the Church of England as well; *Puritanism and Theatre* (Cambridge: The University Press, 1980), 74. But Puritans resented Jonson, who made them his chief target; on 171 Heinemann quotes a contemporary comment about the Puritans: "They quaked at Jonson as by him they pass / Because of Tribulation Wholesome and Ananias . . ." ("Elegy on Randolph's Finger").

28. H&S, 1:2. Unless otherwise noted, facts about Jonson's life comes from this biography.

29. H&S, 1:65–66.

30. H&S, 2:141–42.

31. H&S, 1:3.

32. H&S, 8:582, 610–11.

33. H&S, 8:607, 1437–45.

34. H&S, 8:609–10, 1509–20.

35. H&S, 10:689.

36. H&S, 8:610, 1514–16.

37. Cf. Allan H. Gilbert, *The Symbolic Personages in the Masques of Ben Jonson* (Durham: Duke University Press, 1948) and Stephen Orgel, ed., *Ben Jonson: The Complete Masques* (New Haven: Yale University Press, 1969).

38. H&S, 8:610. 1522–23.

39. H&S, 8:640. 2532–33.

40. H&S, 8:640–41.2534–43.

41. H&S, 1:137.164–65.

42. Induction, 7.

43. H&S, 1:182.

44. H&S, 9:208.

45. The information about the Lady Elizabeth's Men is drawn from G. E. Bentley, *The Jacobean and Caroline Stage* (Oxford: Clarendon Press, 1941–68), 1:176–97.

46. 9:245.

### Chapter 2. The Effect of *Bartholomew Fair*

1. William Armstrong, "Ben Jonson and Jacobean Stagecraft," in *Stratford-upon-Avon Studies I: Jacobean Theatre* (London: Edward Arnold, 1960), 42–61; R. B. Parker, "Themes and Staging of *Bartholomew Fair*," *University of Toronto Quarterly* 39 (1970): 293–309; Eugene Waith, ed. *Bartholomew Fair* (New Haven: Yale University Press, 1971), 205–17.

2. William Blissett, "Your Majesty is Welcome to a Fair," in *The Elizabethan Theatre*, vol. 4, ed. G. R. Hibbard (London: Macmillan, 1974), 86–87. My discussion of the play's effect on its two audiences is indebted to Blissett's reading.

3. H&S, 1:15–16, 38–39; 5:144ff.

4. Blisset, 89–91.

5. Cf. 2.5.145, 2.6.132. 4.4.107, 4.4.135, 4.5.59, 4.6.153.

6. H&S, 8:582.

7. Waith, 211.

8. My discussion is, of course, indebted to Richard Southern's *The Medieval Theatre in the Round*, 2d ed. (London: Faber and Faber, 1975).

9. Ray L. Heffner, Jr., "Unifying Symbols in the Comedy of Ben Jonson," in *Twentieth Century Views*, 142, 145.

10. Cf. Jackson Cope, "*Bartholomew Fair* as Blasphemy," *Renaissance Drama* 8 (1965): 127–52.

11. My discussion of this point has been influenced by G. R. Hibbard's convincing arguments in the "Introduction" to the New Mermaids edition of the play (New York: W. W. Norton, 1977), xxx–xxxi.

12. H&S, 8:597.

13. Ibid.

14. H&S, 10:210–11.

15. H&S, 8:597.

## Chapter 3. The Play's Influence: 1614–1660

1. H&S, 9:196, 208–9, 223–27.

2. H&S, 1:183.

3. G. E. Bentley, *Shakespeare and Jonson* (Chicago: University of Chicago Press, 1945), 1:132–40.

4. In *The Jacobean and Caroline Stage*, G. E. Bentley suggests the play's influence on Middleton, 4:885, 902; Ward, 5:1238; and Shirley, 5:1167. Bentley dismisses the idea that *Bartholomew Fair* influenced Shirley's *The Ball*. When one considers the play's influence, one must also note that *Bartholomew Fair* is the earliest—if indeed it is not the progenitor—of the topographical comedies popular in the 1630s. These plays are Marmion's *Holland's Leaguer* (1631), Shirley's *Hyde Park* (1632), Brome's *Weeding of Covent Garden* (1632), Nabbes's *Covent Garden* (1632), Nabbes's *Tottenham Court* (1633), and Brome's *Sparagus Garden* (1635). See Theodore Miles, "Place-Realism in a Group of Caroline Plays," *Review of English Studies* 18 (1942): 428–40, and Richard H. Perkinson, "Topographical Comedy in the Seventeenth Century," *ELH* 3 (1936): 270–90. Perkinson argues that "The genre [of topographical comedy] owes its inception to Jonson's *Bartholomew Fair*" (272).

5. *The Weeding of Covent Garden* (London: Andrew Crook and Henry Brome, 1658), 2.

6. Other elements in Brome's play which recall *Bartholomew Fair* are discussed in Catherine Shaw's *Richard Brome* (Boston: Twayne, 1980), 75–79.

7. See Bentley, *Jacobean and Caroline Stage* (*supra*, note 4). See also Robert Levine, *A Critical Edition of Thomas Middleton's "The Widow"* (Salzburg: Jacobean Drama Studies, 1975), xxxviii–xxxix; Levine accepts *Bartholomew Fair* as a source.

8. H&S, 10:338–40; David J. Lake, *The Canon of Thomas Middleton's Plays* (London: Cambridge University Press, 1975), 38–43.

9. H&S, 10:338–40; Levine, xxviiiff.

10. Margot Heinemann has an interesting discussion of this scene and its meaning in *Puritanism and Theatre*.

11. *Fucus Histriomastix*, ed. G. C. Moore Smith (Cambridge: The University Press, 1909). Hereafter cited as *FH*.

12. *FH*, ix, gives details about Ward. Moore Smith thinks Fucus like Busy, but hazards no guess on how Ward might have known Jonson's play.

13. *FH*, xii–xiii.

14. *FH*, xiii–xiv.

15. James Shirley, *The Dramatic Works and Poems*, ed. Alexander Dyce (London: John Murray, 1833), vol. 1. R. S. Forsythe, *The Relations of Shirley's Plays to the Elizabethan Drama* (1914; reprint, New York: Benjamin Blom, 1965), agrees that *Bartholomew Fair* was a source for Shirley's *Witty Fair One*, 331, 333.

16. The pamphlet is reprinted in E. A. Horsman's edition of *Bartholomew Fair* (Cambridge, Mass.: Harvard University Press, 1960), 167–69.

17. Although the Folio is dated 1640, its issue was not begun until 1641, H&S, 9:95ff.

18. G. E. Bentley, *Shakespeare and Jonson* (Chicago: University of Chicago Press, 1945), 2:43.

19. Leslie Hotson, *The Commonwealth and Restoration Stage* (New York: Russell and Russell, 1962), gives a good account in chapter 1.

20. Heinemann, 171.

21. I discuss this pamphlet in "Ben Jonson's Poverty," *Biography* 2 (1979): 260–65.

22. All known performances for these years are listed in *Annals of English Drama, 975–1700*, by Alfred Harbage, rev. by Samuel Schoenbaum (London: Methuen, 1964).

23. Hotson, 68–69.

24. Hotson, 8.

25. Hotson, 24.

26. "A Bartholomew Fairing, New, New, New: Sent from the Raised Siege before *Dvblin*, as a Preparatory Present to the Great Thanksgiving-Day" (London, 1649). The pamphlet is clearly Royalist since the Prologue urges readers to "Laugh at old *Nol* [Cromwell], and drink to the *Black Boy* [Charles II]." The pamphlet was inspired by the Royalist loss at Dublin to Cromwell's forces, which were curiously allied with Celtic Catholics.

27. Cf. Jonas Barish's discussion of Busy's characteristic rhetoric in *Ben Jonson and the Language of Prose Comedy* (Cambridge, Mass.: Harvard University Press, 1960), 197–204.

28. *The Dramatic Records of Sir Henry Herbert*, ed. J. Q. Adams (1917; reprint, New York: Benjamin Blom, 1964), 117.

29. Robert Gale Noyes, *Ben Jonson on the English Stage 1660–1776* (1935; reprint, New York: Benjamin Blom, 1966), 223.

30. *The Diary of Samuel Pepys*, ed. Robert Latham et al. (Berkeley and Los Angeles: University of California Press, 1970), 2:174. In this edition William Armstrong argues that this production was *The Play of the Puritan* that I discuss in chapter 4, basing his argument on R. F. Bosher's *The Making of the Restoration Settlement* (New York: Oxford University Press, 1951). But Bosher introduces no new evidence to support such an identification, and I find his conclusion unconvincing. Surely if the September 7 production were *The Play of the Puritan*, Pepys would have mentioned the second Puritan or the different title or the allusions to Baxter.

31. H&S, 1:134.

32. H&S, 8:207. 89ff. The "Venusine" is Horace.

33. H&S, 8:299.

34. See also H&S, 11:584–85. C. J. Sisson, "Ben Jonson of Gresham College," *Times Literary Supplement*, September 21, 1951, p. 604, and Johnston, "Ben Jonson of Gresham College," *Times Literary Supplement*, December 28, 1951, p. 837.

35. H&S, 8:20.

36. H&S, 8:405.

37. H&S, 1:91.

38. H&S, 1:97–98.

39. H&S, 1:211–14.

40. H&S, 9:85–86.

41. H&S, 1:211.

42. H&S, 9:95.

## Chapter 4. *Bartholomew Fair* Restored: 1660–1700

1. Noyes, 222. He gives an almanac of performances on 319ff.

2. For discussions of Restoration audiences and theaters, see Hotson; Allardyce Nicoll, *History of English Drama*, vol. 1 (Cambridge: The University Press, 1955); Robert Hume, *Development of English Drama in the Late Seventeenth Century* (Oxford: Clarendon, 1976); and Hume, ed., *The London Theatre World: 1660–1800* (Carbondale: Southern Illinois University Press, 1980).

3. Cf. *The Jonson Allusion Book (JAB)*, ed. Jesse Franklin Bradley and Joseph Quincy Adams (New Haven: Yale University Press, 1922) for the relevant quotations from these and other critics.

4. John Downes, *Roscius Anglicanus*, ed. Montague Summers (1929; reprint, New York: Benjamin Blom, 1968), 8, 40. Gerald Langbaine, *Momus Triumphans & The Lives and Characters of the English Dramatick Poets* (1699; facsimile, New York: Garland, 1973), in *Lives and Characters*, 77. See also *An Account of the English Dramatick Poets* (1691; facsimile, Los Angeles: William Andrews Clark Memorial Library, 1971), 2 : 287–88.

5. Noyes, 4. See also Bentley, *Shakespeare and Jonson*, 1 : 130ff.

6. Hume, *Development*, 38.

7. John Dryden, *An Essay of Dramatick Poesy* in *The Works of John Dryden* (Berkeley and Los Angeles: University of California Press, 1971), 17 : 21. Unfortunately I was not able to use a complete set of the Berkeley Dryden since it is still being issued. I also have used Montague Summers's ed. of *The Dramatick Works* (London: Nonesuch, 1931). I shall, of course, specify which edition I am using.

8. See *JAB* for typical comments. Cf. Noyes, 5ff., for a discussion of the influence of Jonson's classicism.

9. Dryden, *A Defense of an Essay of Dramatick Poesy*, Berkeley ed., 9 : 6–7.

10. Thomas Brown, *Amusements Serious and Comical* (London: John Nutt, 1700), 1 : 190. "Nuperical" is a neologism meaning "of a recent time; of a time just a little while ago."

11. See Shadwell's Preface to *The Humorists* (1671); see also Edward Howard's Preface to *The Women's Conquest.*

12. Shadwell, Preface to *The Sullen Lovers* in *The Works of Thomas Shadwell*, ed. Montague Summers (London: Fortune Press, 1927), 1 : 11.

13. Dryden, "The Author's Apology for Heroic Poetry and Poetic License," prefaced to *The State of Innocence*, Summers's ed., 2 : 424.

14. Dryden, "Defense of the Epilogue to *Almanazor and Almahide*, or *The Conquest of Grenada, The Second Part*," Summers's ed., 3 : 172.

15. William Congreve, *Letters and Documents*, ed. John C. Hodges (New York: Harcourt, Brace & World, 1964), 181.

16. John Marston, *The Fawn* (Lincoln: University of Nebraska Press, 1965), "To My Equal Reader," 5.

17. Edward Phillips, *Theatrum Poetarum* (1675; reprint, New York: Georg Olms Verlag, 1970), pt. 2, 19–20.

18. Cf. comments in *JAB*, 344, 345, 368, 369, 377, 378, 381, 386, 387, 401, 402, 405, 409, 424, 432.

19. Noyes, 321.

20. Pepys, 2 : 116–17.

21. Downes, 2–8.

22. *The London Stage 1660–1800*, ed. William van Lennep et al. (Carbondale: Southern Illinois University Press, 1965–68), 1 : 28.

23. Downes, 17.

24. Nicoll, 68.

25. Noyes, 224–25.

26. Noyes, 44, 46.

27. Noyes, 44, 107, 174.

28. Noyes, 46–47.

29. Noyes, 107.

30. *A Biographical Dictionary of Actors etc.*, ed. Philip H. Highfill et al., 3 : 493.

31. Noyes never mentions her in a Jonsonian role, nor do I find her cast in any Jonson roles according to *The London Stage.*

32. Noyes, 44–47.

33. Pepys, 2:127, ". . . with my Lady Batten, Mrs. Rebecca Allen, Mrs. Hempson &c., two coaches of us, we went and saw *Bartholmew fayre*, acted very well."

34. *London Stage*, 1:lxix.

35. *Collections of the Massachusetts Historical Society* (Boston: Massachusetts Historical Society, 1868), 4th ser., 8:177–78. The production is also mentioned in *The Diary of the Rev. Henry Newcome*, ed. Thomas Heywood (Manchester: The Chetham Society, 1848), *Remains Historical and Literary [of] Lancaster and Chester*, 18:7–8. Rev. Newcome had written, "Mr Bagshaw dined with mee and told mee a sad story about Mr Baxter beinge silenced in Worcester Dioces, and allso about a play wrein he with other divines were acted. Surely it is great matter of mourneinge before ye Lord. This, even this, is."

36. *Biographical Dictionary*, 3:494.

37. *London Stage*, 1:35.

38. *London Stage*, 1:lxx.

39. Nicoll, 296 and 301, gives the companies' repertoires.

40. George C. D. Odell, *Shakespeare from Betterton to Irving* (1920; reprint, New York: Dover Publications, 1966), 1:24.

41. Nicoll, 343.

42. *London Stage*, 1:156, 225.

43. Noyes, 228–29.

44. Beard, *The Theatre of Gods Judgements* [in two parts], 4th ed. (London: S. I. & M. Hands, 1642–48).

45. *Report on the Manuscripts of the Earl of Egmont* (London: Historical Manuscripts Commission, 1905), 2:24.

46. Southwell, quoted in Morley, 224.

47. Richard Baxter, *Reliquiae Baxterianae* (London: T. Parkhurst, etc., 1696), pt. 3, 84.

48. Noyes, 25.

49. Thomas D'Urfey, *Collin's Walk through London and Westminster* (London: John Bullard, 1690); the trip to the theater is recounted in Canto 3.

### Chapter 5. The Play at Drury Lane: 1700–1735

1. See Noyes, 319ff.

2. Although I agree with Hume's analysis of the audience for the most part, Nicoll's description of the audience in the very first years of the Restoration seems sound. Certainly Hume is correct in his argument that the audience attracted citizens more quickly than Nicoll suggests. See Nicoll, 5ff. and Hume, *Development*, 23ff.

3. Odell, 87.

4. The performance was January 15, 1685; *London Stage*, 1:335.

5. Langbaine, *Lives and Characters*, 77–80.

6. Cf. Hume, *Development*, chapter 9.

7. Odell, 84; cf. Charles Gildon, *A Comparison between the Two Stages* (1702; facsimile, New York: Garland, 1973), 42–44; the passage is very amusing.

8. Noyes, 320–21.

9. *London Stage*, 2.1. 21.

10. Colley Cibber, *An Apology for the Life of Mr. Colley Cibber*, ed. Robert Lowe (1889; facsimile, New York: AMS Press, 1966); the material in vol. 2 includes Anthony Aston's *Supplement* and Edmund Bellchamber's *Memoirs of the Actors and Actresses*: Powell, 2:352–54; Mills, 2:362–64; Verbruggen, 2:354–56; Williams, 1:200, 2:356–57; Mrs.

Mountford, 1:200, 2:313–14; Wilks, 1:235, 2:254–55; Johnson, 2:360–61; Bullock, 2:361–62.

11. Although the 1718 cast list assigns the role to Wilks, a 1720 list assigns it to Wilks, Jr. See my appendix, "Casting of *Bartholomew Fair* in the 18th Century."

12. For all information on casting, see Appendix A. I have compiled this table from the relevant citations in *London Stage*, cross-checked with Noyes.

13. *London Stage*, 2.1. cxv; cf. Gildon, "If they desir'd a Tragedy, they went to Lincolns-Inn-fields; if to Comedy, they flockt to Drury-Lane," 14.

14. *London Stage*, 2.1. xcvi.

15. *London Stage*, 2.1. xxiii and xli.

16. Cibber, 1:321–22.

17. Cibber, 1:322.

18. The account I give of Rich's dealings is a composite one. The primary account is Cibber's, given in the *Apology, passim*, but Cibber is hardly unbiased. The bargain between Rich and Swiney is described in general terms in *London Stage*, 2.1. 129 and in more detail in Brian Dobbs, *Drury Lane* (London: Cassell, 1972), 78–80.

19. Morley, 281.

20. Noyes, 237–39.

21. Noyes, 237–38.

22. Noyes, 237.

23. See Appendix A.

24. *London Stage*, 2.1. liv.

25. Cibber's *Apology* gives an account of how the Triumvirate came into existence, 2:32–60. See also *London Stage*, 2.1.lxxxiff.

26. There is *no* good, clear, and trustworthy account of what happened. The account Cibber gives is hostile and may be distorted, 2:57–72. Dobbs's account in chapter 5, "Triumvirate and Trade Union," is clearer but lacks some of the important details Cibber gives. Nicoll reproduces the relevant documents, 282ff.

27. Cibber, 2:73.

28. Noyes, 322ff.

29. In the August 31, 1708 production, Leigh is named for the role of Crumplin. According to the *OED*, a crumplin is something crumpled such as gingerbread or a deformed person. Either Crumplin is the name of a new character, or it is another name for Joan Trash, the gingerbread woman. Leigh took another woman's role, that of Ursula, in March 1718; Joan Trash, so-named, was played by Mr. Wright in 1731; so a man could plausibly take the role.

30. *London Stage*, 2.1. 281, 361, 456; 2.1. 488, 537, 701.

31. *London Stage*, 2.1. 457.

32. *London Stage*, 2.1. 425; 2.2. 701.

33. *London Stage*, 3.1. 164.

34. *London Stage*, 3.1. 505.

35. Jeremy Collier, *A Short View of the Immorality and Profaneness of the English Stage* (1698; facsimile, Munich: Wilhelm Fink Verlag, 1967), 50. What Collier thinks of *Hamlet* is characteristic:

Had *Shakespear* secur'd this point [of modest behavior] for his young Virgin *Ophelia*, the *Play* had been better contriv'd. Since he was resolv'd to drown the Lady like a Kitten, he should have set her a swimming a little sooner. To keep her alive only to sully her Reputation, and discover the Rankness of her Breath, was very Cruel. (10)

Chapter 6. "Out-o'-the-way, Far-fetched, Perverted Things"

1. Morley, 349ff.

2. Noyes, 5.

3. Noyes, 88.

4. John Brown, *An Estimate of the Manners and Principles of the Times* (1757–58), 1:48.

5. *Dictionary of National Biography.*

6. *The Private Correspondence of David Garrick,* ed. James Boaden (London: Henry Colburn and Richard Bentley, n.d.), 1:146. Noyes corrects Boaden's dating, 243. The other "piece" of which Brown speaks is a tragedy entitled *Armida.*

7. Boaden, 1:146–47.

8. Noyes, 244.

9. *The Letters of David Garrick,* ed. David Little and George Kahrl (Cambridge, Mass.: Harvard University Press, 1963), 2:476–77.

10. *Dictionary of National Biography.* See also Boaden, 1:220.

11. Martha England, *Garrick's Jubilee* (Columbus: Ohio State University Press, 1964), 171.

12. Stuart Tave, "Corbyn Morris: Falstaff, Humor, and Comic Theory in the Eighteenth Century," *Modern Philology* 50 (1952): 102.

13. Noyes, 143–48.

14. Noyes, 197–200.

15. Macklin's letter about the pamphlet was sent to the *General Advertiser* in April 1748 in order to promote his wife's benefit performance. The letter is reproduced in Edmond Malone's edition of *The Plays and Poems of William Shakespeare* (1790; reprint, New York: AMS Press, 1968), vol. 1, pt. 1, 202–6. Malone's refutation follows, vol. 1, pt. 1, 387–414; he concludes that Macklin's slander was "a mere *jeu d'esprit.*"

16. Jonas Barish, "Introduction," *Twentieth Century Views,* 4.

17. Malone, vol. 1, pt. 1, 202–6.

18. Theophilus Cibber, *Lives of the Poets,* rev. Robert Shiells, (1753; reprint, Hildesheim: Georg Olm Verlagsbuchhandlung, 1968), 1:241.

19. Malone, vol. 1, pt. 1, 322.

20. Cf. *The Works of Ben Jonson,* ed. William Gifford (London: W. Bulmer, 1816), 1:cclxvii, cclxxiv, cclxxxi, cclxxxiii.

21. Quoted in Gifford, 1:cii.

22. Gifford, 1:ci.

23. Noyes, 31.

24. Charles Lamb, *Specimens of English Dramatic Poets Who Lived about the Time of Shakespeare* (London: George Bell and Sons, 1890), iv.

25. Lamb, 283.

26. Cf. Gifford, 1:ccxlvix–ccxci, passim.

27. Gifford, cclxix.

28. Gifford, cclxxiv–cclxxv.

29. Gifford, ccxvii–ccxix.

30. Augustus von Schlegel, *Course of Lectures on Dramatic Art and Literature,* trans. John Black, rev. A. J. W. Morrison (1846; reprint, New York: AMS Press, 1973), 461.

31. Schlegel, 463.

32. Schlegel, 464.

33. William Hazlitt, *Lectures on the English Comic Writers* (1891; reprint, New York: Russell and Russell, 1969), 72.

34. *Leigh Hunt's Dramatic Criticism,* ed. Lawrence Huston Houtchens and Carolyn Washburn Houtchens (New York: Columbia University Press, 1949), 122.

35. Schlegel, 461.

36. Hazlitt, 73–74.

37. Hazlitt, 85.

38. Samuel Taylor Coleridge, *Shakespeare, Ben Jonson, Beaumont and Fletcher: Notes and Lectures* (Liverpool: Edward Howell, 1881), 261.

39. Coleridge, 262.

40. Hazlitt, 75.

41. William Wordsworth, *The Prelude,* ed. Jonathan Wordsworth, M. H. Abrams, Stephen Gill (New York: W. W. Norton, 1979), from the 1850 ed., 7:676–81, 706–18, 722–30.

42. *The Prelude,* 262 n.2.

43. *The Letters of Charles Dickens: 1844–1846,* ed. Katherine Tillotson (Oxford: Clarendon Press, 1977), 4:387–91.

44. *Letters of Dickens,* 4:390.

45. *Letters of Dickens,* 4:388–89.

46. *Letters of Dickens,* 4:368–69.

47. Morley, 116.

48. John Addington Symonds, *Ben Jonson* (1886; reprint, New York: AMS Press, 1970).

49. Algernon Swinburne, *A Study of Ben Jonson,* ed. Howard Norland (1889; reprint, Lincoln: University of Nebraska Press, 1969), 60.

50. Swinburne, 61–62.

51. Swinburne, 60–61.

52. Swinburne, xii–xiii.

53. Robert Speaight, *William Poel and the Elizabethan Revival* (Cambridge, Mass.: Harvard University Press, 1954), 116.

54. Speaight, 192–93, 116, 127.

55. Speaight, Appendix 1, compiled by Allan Gomme, 279ff.

56. In addition to contemporary reviews, I have found information about the production in Noyes, 245, and H&S, 9:249.

57. London *Times,* June 28, 1921.

58. Noyes, 245.

59. Ejner Jensen, "Lamb, Poel, and Our Postwar Theater: Elizabethan Revivals," Renaissance Drama, n.s., 9 (1978): 224.

60. Jensen, 225.

61. Jensen, 226.

### Chapter 7. The Rebirth of *Bartholomew Fair*

1. *Manchester Guardian,* June 28, 1921; *Nation and Athenaeum,* July 2, 1921.

2. *Mercury* (London) 4 (1921); Noyes regards this as an uninformed review and says Turner "completely misunderstood Jonson's attitude toward Puritanism when he remarked that Ben Jonson 'did not concern himself with the Puritan principle at all'" (245). In fact, Turner simply says that Jonson failed to deal with the central principles of Puritan theology and thought the faith "mere cunning hypocrisy." Turner's point seems a valid one; certainly Jonson did not overestimate the intellectual rigor of Puritan thought!

3. *Manchester Guardian,* June 28, 1921.

4. *Nation and Athenaeum,* July 2, 1921; London *Times,* June 28, 1921.

5. London *Times*, June 28, 1921.

6 *Manchester Guardian*, June 28, 1921; *Nation and Athenaeum*, July 2, 1921.

7. H&S, 9:249.

8. Cambridge *Daily News*, March 4, 1947.

9. Cambridge *Daily News*, March 12, 1947.

10. Cf. London *Times*, July 16, 1953, for Festival Players production; information on the Dublin production comes from an interview of Arthur Colby Sprague by Carol Carlisle, which Professor Carlisle was kind enough to pass along to me in a letter, February 25, 1981.

11. Letter from Professor Carlisle, February 25, 1981.

12. Newcastle *Courier*, December 2, 1970.

13. Cambridge *Evening News*, March 7, 1977, gives an account of the problems.

14. Cambridge *Evening News*, March 9, 1977.

15. Cambridge *Daily News*, November 26, 1955.

16. Cambridge *Daily News*, November 26, 1955. Given the further developments in Miller's career, the reviewer's opinion is particularly interesting:

> It is fortunate that copper-headed zany, Jonathan Miller, is touched with natural brilliance as a comic because he gives an appallingly slip-shod performance as the madman, Troubleall. I did not understand one single word he spoke from the beginning to end of the evening.
>
> Yet he made me laugh louder and longer than anyone else. . . . Mr. Miller clucks insanely like a hen-coop raided by a fox, he drums lunatic cadenzas with his naked toes, and the way in which he swathes himself round with a cloak is the most alarmingly comic thing I have seen in Cambridge.
>
> Critical laurels have always been royally ignored by Jonathan Miller, who had, perhaps wisely, determined his career. But the fact remains that he is a natural comedian, and natural comedians are almost as rare as unicorns.

17. Information on this production comes form the records kept at the Shakespeare Centre Library in Stratford-upon-Avon.

18. *Manchester Guardian*, July 29, 1959.

19. Information comes from reviews in the London *Times*, August 31, 1966; the *Observer Weekend Review*, September 4, 1966; and the *Daily Mail*, August 31, 1966. The season was sponsored by the *Daily Mail*; it was the group's "first major non-Shakespearian venture."

20. *Daily Mail*, August 31, 1966.

21. "Stage History from 1660," in the *Riverside Shakespeare*, ed. G. Blakemore Evans (Boston: Houghton Mifflin, 1974), 1816.

22. *Observer Weekend Review*, September 4, 1966.

23. Information on the Old Vic productions comes from Devine's promptbook and the production files at the Old Vic Theatre.

24. Information on the Bristol Old Vic production comes from the production files at the Bristol Old Vic Theatre. I was unable to see the promptbook.

25. Information on the Radio 3 production comes from the *Radio Times*, July 4, 1968.

26. Information on the Royal Shakespeare Company production comes from the promptbook and production files at the Shakespeare Centre Library.

27. Information on the Nottingham production comes from the production files at the Nottinghamshire County Library and an interview with George Parfitt. I was unable to see the promptbook.

28. Information on the Round House production comes from the promptbook and

production files at the Round House and interviews with Peter Barnes, Malcolm Taylor, and Thelma Holt.

29. Information on the Young Vic production comes from the promptbook and production files at the Young Vic and an interview with Michael Bogdanov.

30. Irving Wardle, *The Theatres of George Devine* (London: Jonathan Cape, 1978), 66.

31. Wardle, 64.

32. Wardle, 115.

33. London *Times*, August 24, 1950.

34. John Arden, *To Present the Pretence* (London: Eyre Methuen, 1977), 32–33.

35. London *Times*, December 19, 1950.

36. Wardle, 134–35.

37. *Stage*, August 9, 1966.

38. *Sunday Telegraph*, October 26, 1969.

39. Birmingham *Post*, November 8, 1969.

40. The other review is in the Birmingham *Post*, October 31, 1969.

41. *Sunday Telegraph*, November 2, 1969.

42. London *Times*, October 31, 1969.

43. *Queen*, November 26, 1969.

44. D. A. N. Jones, *The Listener*, September 26, 1968.

45. *The Listener*, November 6, 1969.

46. London *Times*, November 8, 1969.

47. Ejner Jensen, *Educational Theatre Journal* 28 (1976): 558.

48. Ibid.

49. Ibid., 558–59.

50. Gillian Reynolds, *Plays and Players* 25:11 (August 1978): 16.

51. London *Times*, August 4, 1978. On the subject of Barnes and Jonson, see also Bernard F. Dukore, *The Theatre of Peter Barnes* (London: Heinemann, 1981), chapter 6, "Editings and Adaptations."

52. London *Times*, August 4, 1978. The detail about Claridge's performance is from Michael Gearin-Tosh's rehearsal diary, preserved in the production files at the Round House.

53. Gillian Reynolds, *Plays and Players* 26:1 (October 1978): 33; London *Times*, August 4, 1978.

# Bibliography

Adams, Joseph Quincy, ed. *The Dramatic Records of Sir Henry Herbert.* 1917. Reprint. New York: Benjamin Blom, 1964.

————, and Jesse Franklin Bradley, eds. *The Jonson Allusion Book.* New Haven: Yale University Press, 1922.

Arden, John. *To Present the Pretence.* London: Eyre Methuen, 1977.

Armstrong, William. "Ben Jonson and Jacobean Stagecraft." In *Stratford-upon-Avon Studies I: Jacobean Theatre*, 42–61. London: Edward Arnold, 1960.

Baird, Bil. *The Art of the Puppet.* New York: Ridge Press, 1973.

Barish, Jonas. *Ben Jonson and the Language of Prose Comedy.* Cambridge, Mass.: Harvard University Press, 1960.

————, ed. Introduction to *Ben Jonson: Twentieth Century Views*. Englewood Cliffs, N.J.: Prentice-Hall, 1963.

"A Bartholomew Fairing, New, New, New: Sent from the Raised Siege before *Dvblin*, as a Preparatory Present to the Great Thanksgiving-Day." London, 1649. Microfilm.

Baxter, Richard. *Reliquiae Baxterianae.* London, 1696. Microfilm.

Beard, Thomas. *The Theatre of Gods Judgements* [in two parts]. 4th ed. London, 1642–48. Microfilm.

Beaurline, L. A. *Jonson and Elizabethan Comedy.* San Marino: Huntington Library, 1978.

Bentley, G. E. *The Jacobean and Caroline Stage.* 7 vols. Oxford: Clarendon Press, 1941–68.

————. *Shakespeare and Jonson.* 2 vols. Chicago: University of Chicago Press, 1945.

Blissett, William. "Your Majesty Is Welcome to a Fair." *Elizabethan Theatre* 4 (Toronto: Macmillan, 1974): 80–105.

Bosher, R. F. *The Making of the Restoration Settlement.* New York: Oxford University Press, 1951.

Brome, Richard. *The Weeding of Covent Garden.* London, 1658. Microform.

Brown, John. *An Estimate of the Manners and Principles of the Times.* 2d ed. Vol. 1. London, 1757–58.

Brown, Thomas. *Amusements Serious and Comical.* Vol. 1. London, 1700. Microfilm.

Chambers, E. K. *Mediaeval Stage.* 2 vols. Oxford: Clarendon Press, 1903.

Cibber, Colley. *An Apology for the Life of Mr. Colley Cibber,* with Anthony Aston's *Supplement* and Edmund Bellchamber's *Memoirs of the Actors and Actresses.* 2 vols. Edited by Robert Lowe. 1889. Reprint. New York: AMS Press, 1966.

Cibber, Theophilus. *Lives of the Poets.* Vol. 1. Revised by Robert Shiells. 1753. Reprint. Hildesheim: Georg Olm Verlagsbuchhandlung, 1968.

Coleridge, Samuel Taylor. *Shakespeare, Ben Jonson, Beaumont and Fletcher: Notes and Lectures.* Liverpool: Edward Howell, 1881.

*Collections of the Massachusetts Historical Society,* 4th series, vol. 8. Boston: Massachusetts Historical Society, 1868.

Collier, Jeremy. *A Short View of the Immortality and Profaneness of the English Stage.* 1698. Reprint. Munich: Wilhelm Fink Verlag, 1967.

Congreve, William. *Letters and Documents.* Edited by John C. Hodges. New York: Harcourt, Brace & World, 1964.

Cope, Jackson. "*Bartholomew Fair* as Blasphemy." *Renaissance Drama* 8 (1965): 127–52.

Dekker, Thomas. *The Dramatic Works of Thomas Dekker.* Vol. 2. Edited by Fredson Bowers. Cambridge: The University Press, 1953–61.

Dessen, Alan. *Jonson's Moral Comedy.* Evanston: Northwestern University Press, 1971.

Dickens, Charles. *The Letters of Charles Dickens: 1844–1846.* Vol. 4. Edited by Katherine Tillotson. Oxford: Clarendon Press, 1977.

Dobbs, Brian. *Drury Lane.* London: Cassell, 1972.

Downes, John. *Roscius Anglicanus.* Edited by Montague Summers. 1929. Reprint. New York: Benjamin Blom, 1968.

Dryden, John. *The Dramatick Works.* Vol. 2. Edited by Montague Summers. London: Nonesuch, 1931–32.

———. *The Works of John Dryden.* Vols. 9 and 17. Edited by Edward Niles Hooker and H. T. Swedenberg, Jr. Berkeley and Los Angeles: University of California Press, 1956–    .

Dukore, Bernard F. *The Theatre of Peter Barnes.* London: Heinemann, 1981.

Durant, Will, and Ariel Durant. *The Age of Reason Begins.* Vol. 7 of *The Story of Civilization.* New York: Simon and Schuster, 1961.

Eliot, T. S. *Selected Essays, 1917–1932.* New York: Harcourt, Brace & World, 1934.

Enck, John J. *Jonson and the Comic Truth.* Madison: University of Wisconsin Press, 1966.

England, Martha. *Garrick's Jubilee.* Columbus: Ohio State University Press, 1964.

Forsythe, R. S. *The Relations of Shirley's Plays to the Elizabethan Drama.* 1914. Reprint. New York: Benjamin Blom, 1965.

Garrick, David. *The Letters of David Garrick.* Vol. 2. Edited by David Little and George Kahrl. London: Oxford University Press, 1963.

———. *The Private Correspondence of David Garrick.* Edited by James Boaden. Vol. 1. London: Henry Colburn and Richard Bentley, 1821.

Gilbert, Allan H. *The Symbolic Personages in the Masques of Ben Jonson.* Durham: Duke University Press, 1948.

Gildon, Charles. *A Comparison between the Two Stages.* 1702. Reprint. New York: Garland, 1973.

Harbage, Alfred. *Annals of English Drama, 975–1700.* Revised by Samuel Schoenbaum. London: Methuen, 1964.

Hazlitt, William. *Lectures on the English Comic Writers.* 1891. Reprint. New York: Russell and Russell, 1969.

Heffner, Ray L., Jr. "Unifying Symbols in the Comedy of Ben Jonson." In *Ben Jonson: Twentieth Century Views.* 133–46. See Barish, 1963.

Heinemann, Margot. *Puritanism and Theatre.* Cambridge: The University Press, 1980.

Highfill, Philip H., et al., ed. *A Biographical Dictionary of Actors.* 8 vols. to date. Carbondale: Southern Illinois University Press, 1973–.

Hotson, Leslie. *The Commonwealth and Restoration Stage.* New York: Russell and Russell, 1962.

Howard, Edward. *The Womens Conquest* London, 1671. Microfilm.

Hume, Robert. *Development of English Drama in the Late Seventeenth Century.* Oxford: Clarendon Press, 1976.

———, ed. *The London Theatre World: 1660–1800.* Carbondale: Southern Illinois University Press, 1980.

Hunt, Leigh. *Leigh Hunt's Dramatic Criticism.* Edited by Laurence Huston Houtchens and Carolyn Washburn Houtchens. New York: Columbia University Press, 1949.

Jackson, Gabriele. *Vision and Judgment in Ben Jonson's Drama.* New Haven: Yale University Press, 1968.

Jensen, Ejner. "Bartholomew Fair." *Educational Theatre Journal* 28 (1976): 558.

———. "Lamb, Poel, and Our Postwar Theater: Elizabethan Revivals," *Renaissance Drama*, n.s., 9 (1978): 211–34.

Jonson, Ben. *Bartholomew Fair.* Edited by G. R. Hibbard. New York: W. W. Norton, 1977.

———. *Bartholomew Fair.* Edited by E. A. Horsman. Cambridge, Mass.: Harvard University Press, 1960.

———. *Bartholomew Fair.* Edited by Edward B. Partridge. Lincoln: University of Nebraska Press, 1964.

———. *Bartholomew Fair.* Edited by Eugene M. Waith. New Haven: Yale University Press, 1963.

———. *Complete Masques.* Edited by Stephen Orgel. New Haven: Yale University Press, 1969.

———. *Works.* Edited by William Gifford. 9 vols. London: W. Bulmer, 1816.

———. *Works.* Edited by C. H. Herford, Percy Simpson, and Evelyn Simpson. 11 vols. Oxford: Clarendon Press, 1925–52.

Johnston, George Burke. "Ben Jonson of Gresham College." *Times Literary Supplement* December 28, 1951, p. 837.

Knoll, Robert. *Ben Jonson's Plays: An Introduction.* Lincoln: University of Nebraska Press, 1964.

Lake, David J. *The Canon of Thomas Middleton's Plays.* London: Cambridge University Press, 1975.

Lamb, Charles. *Specimens of English Dramatic Poets Who Lived about the Time of Shakspeare.* London: George Bell and Sons, 1890.

Langbaine, Gerald. *An Account of the English Dramatick Poets.* Vol. 2. 1691. Reprint. Los Angeles: William Andrews Clark Memorial Library, 1971.

———. *Momus Triumphans & The Lives and Characters of the English Dramatick Poets.* 1688. Reprint. New York: Garland, 1973.

Lennep, William van, et al., eds. *The London Stage 1660–1800.* 5 vols. in 11. Carbondale: Southern Illinois University Press, 1965–68.

Levine, Robert, ed. *A Critical Edition of Thomas Middleton's "The Widow."* Salzburg: Salzburg Studies in Jacobean Drama, 1975.

Marston, John. *The Fawn.* Edited by Gerald A. Smith. Lincoln: University of Nebraska Press, 1965.

Miles, Theodore. "Place-Realism in a Group of Caroline Plays," *Review of English Studies* 18 (1942): 428–40.

M[oore], N[orman]. "Rahere." *Dictionary of National Biography* (1921–22).

Morley, Henry. *Memoirs of Bartholomew Fair.* London: Frederick Warne, 1859.

Neale, J. E. *Queen Elizabeth I.* New York: Doubleday Anchor, 1957.

Newcome, Henry. *The Diary of the Rev. Henry Newcome.* Edited by Thomas Heywood. In *Remains Historical and Literary [of] Lancaster and Chester,* vol. 18. Manchester: The Chetham Society, 1848.

Nicoll, Allardyce. *History of English Drama.* 6 vols. Cambridge: The University Press, 1952–59.

Noyes, Robert Gale. *Ben Jonson on the English Stage 1660–1776.* 1935. Reprint. New York: Benjamin Blom, 1966.

Odell, George C. D. *Shakespeare from Betterton to Irving.* Vol. 1. 1920. Reprint. New York: Dover Publications, 1966.

Parker, R. B. "Themes and Staging of *Bartholomew Fair.*" *University of Toronto Quarterly* 39 (1970): 293–309.

Partridge, E. B. "Jonson's Large and Unique View of Life." *Elizabethan Theatre* 4 (Toronto: Macmillan, 1974): 143–67.

Pepys, Samuel. *The Diary of Samuel Pepys.* Vol. 2. Edited by Robert Latham, William Matthews et al. Berkeley: University of California Press, 1970.

Perkinson, Richard H. "Topographical Comedy in the Seventeenth Century." *ELH* 3 (1936): 270–90.

Phillips, Edward. *Theatrum Poetarum.* 1675. Reprint. Hildesheim: Georg Olms Verlag, 1970.

*Report on the Manuscripts of the Earl of Egmont.* Vol. 2. London: Historical Manuscripts Commission, 1905.

Schlegel, Augustus von. *Course of Lectures on Dramatic Art and Literature.* Translated by John Black. Revised by A. J. W. Morrison. 1846. Reprint. New York: AMS Press, 1973.

Shadwell, Thomas. *The Works of Thomas Shadwell.* Vol. 1. Edited by Montague Summers. London: Fortune Press, 1927.

Shakespeare, William. *The Plays and Poems of William Shakespeare.* Vol. 1. Edited by Edmond Malone. 1790. Reprint. New York: AMS Press, 1968.

———. *Riverside Shakespeare.* Edited by G. Blakemore Evans. Boston: Houghton Mifflin, 1974.

Shaw, Catherine. *Richard Brome.* Boston: Twayne, 1980.

Shirley, James. *The Dramatic Works and Poems.* Vol. 1. Edited by Alexander Dyce. London: John Murray, 1833.

Sisson, C. J. "Ben Jonson of Gresham College." *Times Literary Supplement*, September 21, 1951, p. 604.

Southern, Richard. *The Medieval Theatre in the Round.* 2d ed. London: Faber and Faber, 1975.

Speaight, George. *The History of the English Puppet Theatre.* New York: John de Graff, n.d.

Speaight, Robert. *William Poel and the Elizabethan Revival.* Cambridge, Mass.: Harvard University Press, 1954.

Swinburne, Algernon. *A Study of Ben Jonson.* Edited by Howard Norland. 1889. Reprint. Lincoln: University of Nebraska Press, 1969.

Symonds, John Addington. *Ben Jonson.* 1886. Reprint. New York: AMS Press, 1970.

Tave, Stuart. "Corbyn Morris: Falstaff, Humor, and Comic Theory in the Eighteenth Century." *Modern Philology* 50 (1952): 102–15.

Teague, Frances. "Ben Jonson's Poverty." *Biography* 2 (1979): 260–65.

Thayer, C. G. *Ben Jonson: Studies in the Plays.* Norman: University of Oklahoma Press, 1963.

Townsend, Freda L. *Apologie for Bartholomew Fayre.* New York: Modern Language Association, 1947.

Urfey, Thomas D'. *Collin's Walk through London and Westminster.* London, 1690. Microfilm.

Ward, Robert. *Fucus Histriomastix.* Edited by G. C. Moore Smith. Cambridge: The University Press, 1909.

Wardle, Irving. *The Theatres of George Devine.* London: Jonathan Cape, 1978.

Weld, John S. "Christian Comedy: *Volpone.*" *Studies in Philology* 51 (1954): 172–93.

Wilson, Edmund. "Morose Ben Jonson." In *Ben Jonson: Twentieth Century Views*, 60–74. See Barish, 1963.

Wolf, William D. *Jacobean Drama Studies: The Reform of the Fallen World.* Salzburg: Salzburg Studies in English Literature, 1973.

Wordsworth, William. *The Prelude.* Edited by Jonathan Wordsworth, M. H. Abrams, Stephen Gill. New York: W. W. Norton, 1979.

# Index